Dedicated to Reverend Father John Newman (deceased) former Parish Priest of the Diocese of Cairns who was passionately committed to nurturing and encouraging the Baptismal vocation of all Catholics to live and witness for Christ, and also dedicated to all Priests and Religious who generously supported the Gulf Mission for most of the last century.

Any profits from the sale of this book will be donated to support the Gulf Savannah Parish of the Diocese of Cairns.

First published in 2020 by Barrallier Books Pty Ltd,
trading as Echo Books

Registered Office: 35—37 Gordon Avenue, West Geelong, Victoria 3220,
Australia.

www.echobooks.com.au

Copyright ©Peter de Haas

Creator: de Haas, Peter: Author.

Title: A Practical Field Guide for Bush Catholics... and *bushed*
Catholics

ISBN: 9780648554066 Paperback

A catalogue record for this
book is available from the
National Library of Australia

**NATIONAL
LIBRARY**
OF AUSTRALIA

Book layout and design by Peter Gamble, Canberra.
Set in Garamond Premier Pro Display, 12/17 and Garamond Premier Pro
Semibold Display

www.echobooks.com.au

Nihil Obstat: Rev. Neil Muir

Imprimatur: Most Rev. James Foley, Bishop of Cairns 15th July 2019

The *nihil obstat* and *imprimatur* are official declarations that a book or pamphlet is free of doctrinal or moral errors. No implication is contained therein that those who have granted the *nihil obstat* and *imprimatur* agree with the contents, opinions or statements expressed.

Biblical references are from the New Revised Standard Version.

A PRACTICAL FIELD GUIDE FOR BUSH CATHOLICS...

and *bushed* Catholics

Peter de Haas

CONTENTS

FOREWORD

I write this within days of returning from ministry in the Gulf: A fine family Baptism and Confirmation at Normanton and then Mass with the community in Croydon.

This was perhaps my last visit before retirement. It reminded me of many previous visits going back to 1992 when I *went bush* as far as Lawn Hill Gorge, with Fr John Butcher (1937-2016). As I recall there was very little sealed road then, beyond Mt Garnet and even the stretch between Ravenshoe and Mt Garnet was a narrow one lane bitumen road. Some of these dangerous narrow sections are still in the middle regions on the road to Normanton.

I shared with Deacon Peter de Haas and Sr Irene Harrison rsj on words from Fr John Flynn (1932-2008) who for many years had worked the Gulf Ministry. There is a point, and I identified it on my return the other day, somewhere mid-way between the *Forty Mile Scrub* (now sadly almost destroyed by bush fire) and Mt Garnet on those long straight stretches where we first glimpse the western side of the Tablelands and have a sense that you are *almost home*. John Flynn himself reflected that on his returns from the haunting loneliness of the Gulf country, when you got to some point along that road, it was *like waking up from a dream.*

Irene and Peter say they have had very similar experiences along that road.

I trust what Peter writes in the following pages will awaken something of that dream in those who read it and bring a sense of deep gratitude for the beauty, indeed the *greatness of God* which can penetrate our souls anywhere and at any time.

Peter. Thank you for these reflections. May this be a graced experience to all who read it.

Yours truly in Christ,
+ **James Foley**
BISHOP OF CAIRNS
4th October 2019

Sometimes when travelling through vast stretches of dried-out country in the Gulf Savannah, months after the wet season, we come across a body of water where life abounds, like an oasis...or a treasure hidden in the field.

PREFACE

The Kingdom of God is like a treasure hidden in a field ...
(Matt 13:44)

If you were baptised as a Catholic, and—for whatever reason—now find yourself separated from the mainstream parish and liturgical life of the Church, then this book might just be for you. Perhaps you are one of thousands of isolated Catholics living in rural and remote areas of Australia, miles from the nearest church which, in any case, is only rarely visited by a Priest, Deacon or Religious. Or are you one of so many Catholics who have *tried* the Church, have found it spiritually unsatisfying and have just stopped going?

If either of these isolating circumstances aligns with your personal lived experience, are you, nevertheless, still spiritually restless? Are you still seeking and yearning for a deeper meaning for your life through a richer Catholic spirituality, or for a spiritual *home*? Perhaps you have searched repeatedly in various bookshops or on Google, or spoken with others, but found yourself overwhelmed by the sheer number of opinions about religion and spirituality, not really knowing where to turn (one of the meanings of *bushed*, the other is *exhausted*).

For those who are still seeking, I am cautiously optimistic you will find something useful or helpful in this *field guide*. Through some of the practices in this book countless thousands throughout the centuries have found themselves drawn into deeper, freer and more life-giving relationships with God ... the God who is always coming towards us!

The idea to write this practical guide slowly emerged from my own reflections on many pastoral encounters with isolated Catholics (and other Christians) in the Australian outback, specifically in Far North Queensland. I thought that an easy-to-read practical guide designed to support and nurture a genuine Catholic spirituality might be helpful, not only for those in the outback but also for those experiencing other forms of isolation from the Church.

This guide is, above all, an *invitation to freely explore* with an open mind and heart, rather than laying out a set of rules to be followed. Such freedom is a key attribute of the Kingdom of God which Jesus proclaimed. Consequently, *Thy Kingdom Come* is a pivotal chapter of this book, seeking to introduce the radical nature of the Kingdom of God inaugurated by Jesus as: ... *life free from the reign of all those forces that enslave humanity ... the sphere of life where God's spirit is in control.*[1] In this space, we discover a much more expansive, yet very inclusive, vision of what it really means to be Church.

Finally, it seems intuitive that God must first be found **within** in order to make any external religious actions either worthwhile or meaningful. As far as I can ascertain, there is no book just like this, so I humbly offer this work to you with my prayers and hopes that it will be of some assistance to find God within **you**, the only *treasure hidden in the field* that is really worth finding.

---

1   J. Kirk, *What is Mission? Theological Explorations* (Minneapolis: Fortress Press, 2000) 29

About the Author

Since 2004, I have lived in Ravenshoe with my wife Angela, and our adult daughter, Alicia, who has some disabilities but many more abilities. Ravenshoe is on the southern end of the Atherton Tablelands, Far North Queensland, about two hour's drive from Cairns.

After completing a formation program, and after extensive discernment, I was ordained as a Permanent Deacon in the Diocese of Cairns in July 2010. Previously, I had professional careers in the Army, public service and private sector and with my family, have lived and worked in various cities across Australia.

Since Ordination, and together with my family as part of a Rural Ministries Team, I have been providing pastoral and spiritual support to the parishioners of the vast Gulf Savannah Parish as well as to cattle station families and communities affected by wildfires, the GFC, live-export ban, and a long-running drought. This Parish, which extends over 900 km to the Northern Territory border and is between 200-400 km across, is sparsely populated with small isolated towns and a large number of cattle stations.

It is this lived experience, and the insights and reflections from the wonderful people encountered *along the track* in these rural and remote areas, which forms the genesis and inspiration for this book

ACKNOWLEDGMENTS

I gratefully acknowledge the support (and forbearance) of my wife, Angela, over the two plus years that it has taken to produce this book. It started as a small idea, which seemed quite innocuous, but then steadily grew into something much larger than I had anticipated. I admit this has also happened with some other projects of mine.

For their valuable and insightful guidance and comments on various stages of the working drafts, the following people are acknowledged with heartfelt thanks: Fr. Laurie Timms, OCarm., Fr. Gerry O'Connor, Sr. Irene Harrison, Lesley Newman, Judy Wilcox, Greg and Robyn Byrnes, Michael McAuliffe, Fr. Nathan McKay, Fr. Paul Rodwell, Fr. Frank Gordon and Fr. Neil Muir.

A very special *thank-you* to my sister, Veronique Hambling, artist, who, inspired by the concept and some key contents of this book, very kindly transformed her inspirations into the evocative illustrations contained herein.

A further special *thank-you* to my nephew Malcolm McKaskill (Facebook–Mal McKaskill Photography), who very kindly, and very professionally, produced digital images of the original illustrations.

Michael Magee's shanty may have looked something like this? People of the bush have always been very resilient and inventive in using whatever materials are at hand to provide for their basic needs: like shelter, food and water. Is it also possible for anyone to construct a 'spiritual shanty'?

INTRODUCTION

Why this Field Guide?

Context and Genesis

> *On the outer Barcoo where the churches are few,*
> *And men of religion are scanty,*
> *On a road never cross'd 'cept by folk that are lost,*
> *One Michael Magee had a shanty.*

> (From *A Bush Christening*,
> by 'Banjo' Paterson, 1893)

A Bush Christening was written some 17 years after the last resident priest left the then fledgling town of Georgetown, located approximately 380 km west of Cairns, today about 6 hours by road. Opening this poem, the verse above captures the essence of the real and continuing isolation of people in the bush from those spiritual and pastoral supports that city and town-based parishioners mostly take for granted, and have easy and timely access to.

Catholics scattered across the vast and remote region which is now known as the Gulf Savannah Parish of the Diocese of Cairns have only very rarely had the opportunity to participate regularly in the sacramental or liturgical life of the Church, or to have access to a Priest, Deacon or Religious for spiritual or pastoral support. This was the situation for most of the last century when priests based closer to Cairns visited what was then known as the *Gulf Mission* only once or twice per year. In recent memory, these priests included: Monsignor Maurice Walsh and Fathers David McKenzie, John Flynn, Pat Jones and John Butcher (now all deceased).

The Gulf Savannah Parish was officially formed in 1996 and dedicated to St. Paul the Evangelist. Fr. Gerald O'Connor became its first Parish Priest and over much of the next decade did regular and demanding circuits through this vast Parish to provide monthly access to Mass and the other Sacraments. Following his retirement, the then Parish Priest in Ravenshoe, Fr. Hilary Flynn, also became Parish Priest of Gulf Savannah Parish and subsequently, from 2015 when Fr. Flynn was moved to Tully Parish, I was requested to work in both Ravenshoe and Gulf Savannah Parishes by Bishop James Foley. At the time of writing, Fr. Laurie Timms, OCarm., has responsibility for pastoral oversight of the Gulf Savannah Parish.

Since the retirement of Fr. O'Connor, parishioners living in the townships within the Gulf Savannah Parish have had access to Mass, on average, about 8-9 times per year. In addition, ongoing pastoral and spiritual support within this Parish has been provided for many years by Sister Irene Harrison, rsj, being joined in 2010 by myself and my family. This support includes providing Liturgies of the Word— with or without Communion—and baptisms, marriages and funerals as appropriate, as well as preparing children (and adults) for the Sacraments.

From this brief history, it should be very clear that entire generations of Catholics in this vast region have experienced a completely different way of *being Catholic*, with much more reliance on developing ways of nurturing faith *personally* rather than *communally*.

It is for those who have inherited, or now find themselves living, this tradition—whether in this Parish or in any of the other vast rural and remote parishes across Australia—that this book is predominantly (but not exclusively) written. May this guide both **validate** and be of some assistance to enrich and nurture your lived experience and your individual journeys in faith towards God.

We might compare this to growing beef which mostly happens out in the paddock and not in the yards where cattle are mustered for herd maintenance. Our spiritual lives are a bit like that, aren't they? Most of the growing and nurturing must take place in the everyday circumstances in which we find ourselves, especially if we are isolated on a remote property somewhere in the outback. If we intentionally seek and allow this, then when we *do* have the opportunity to gather together and participate in the Mass or other communal liturgies, they have the potential to be much deeper and richer experiences. We will each have something to bring and to share with one another—the insights and lived experience of people genuinely seeking God, and trying to find meaning in whatever situations we find ourselves in.

How would you describe your personal lived experience of 'being Catholic?

How connected do you feel to the Church, or to other Catholics?

Please remember, however, that this guide is very much in the nature of an *invitation* and not a prescription, nor a set of rules or procedures which have to be followed. You, the reader, are invited to consider the various suggestions and practices which are outlined and apply them as appropriate into your own particular and unique circumstances, those which will have been shaped by all that has gone before, and also where you are at spiritually when this guide lands in your mail box or on your kitchen table. Only you and God together can determine the way in which you might personally use and apply this guide, either in whole or in part.

This picture of two cattle peering tentatively back at the broken down yards might mirror the experience of some 'bushed Catholics' looking tentatively at what they perceive to be the ruins of the church where they once belonged.

Are You a Bushed Catholic?

A very wise theologian once wrote that God must first be found *within* us in order to make any external religious actions either worthwhile or meaningful. May this guide be of some help to encounter more fully the God within. Perhaps it might, therefore, also be useful for *bushed Catholics*, those who have lost their way somewhat and find themselves spiritually isolated, and even disoriented, in altogether different sorts of places—in what can feel like a private spiritual wilderness, feeling cut off or distant from the Church.

We must also acknowledge and squarely face up to the fact that far too many people have been deeply, deeply hurt by the actions of some of its representatives, or otherwise alienated by an unkind word or a lack of patience or understanding. On a larger scale, the Church can come across as having lost its way to the extent that it is very hard, if not impossible, for people to encounter Christ. This is especially true when the Church appears to be just another very impersonal and bureaucratic institution, concerned more with rules, authority and power than with compassion and pastoral concern for people. So, many people just leave, often hurt or disillusioned.

Back to Basics?

This is a great pity because what all Catholics are first and foremost called to be is the people, or, better still, the *children* of God, trying to support one another in living the Greatest Commandments, the two which sum up the entire Bible:

> 'You shall love the Lord your God with all your heart, and with all your soul, and with all your mind.' This is the greatest and first commandment. And a second is like it: 'You shall love your neighbour as yourself.' (Matthew 22:37-39).

As sons and daughters of God, the Catholic Church teaches that we are all one family in Christ no matter where (or when) we live, so long as we each strive to live these two commandments.[2] The term *family* is very appropriate because, as we shall see later, a family can also make Jesus' church fully present in their particular local setting.

---

2   Adapted from the Vatican II document, *Lumen Gentium: Light of the Nations*, 51

> *'The Church is a family ... and a family is a church ...'*
>
> *What do you think about this statement?*
>
> *How might it change your sense of what it means to be Catholic?*

In the first decades after Jesus' resurrection, Christianity became manifest in family households long before separate church buildings were constructed. (Interestingly, these *home churches* were often led by women.) So, these homely settings are close to the *original Way*, that which Jesus left behind. Some might reasonably ask whether even He could have foreseen how His movement would become so institutionalised. This vision of *church as a family* is an important foundation for the development of this field guide.

In early 2017, Archbishop Julian Porteous of Hobart gave a statement on evangelisation for the National Association of Deacons, which included the following:

> We need people to be formed in faith, who enter more deeply into a personal relationship with the Lord, deepening their own prayer life, their attentiveness to Scripture, their desire to live their lives in deep personal union with Christ – who then want to reach out and help others discover what they've discovered, help them find the treasure they've discovered in Christ.[3]

May this guide be of some assistance for all of us, not only in seeking a deeper and very personal relationship with Jesus the Christ, but also in making Him real and present for others who are yearning for lasting meaning, and for some hope and love.

What is in this book?

This is a very good question, but one that has been difficult to grapple with from the outset. Matters of Catholic faith, religion, spirituality and practice are each vast, limitless topics on which entire

---

3   Quoted in the National Association of Deacons Australia newsletter of January 2017, page 7 or via the following link: https://www.ausdeacons.org.au/eNews/eNEWSletter_Jan_2017.pdf .

libraries have already been written. So I have tried to be realistic and very modest in what can reasonably be achieved herein, and I respectfully request similar expectations from you, the reader.

Of course, by its very nature, a spiritual guide can only describe possible pathways, but never fully reveal the destination. Also, there just isn't a single step-by-step instruction manual to a deeper faith. Pope Benedict is reported to have told a reporter once that there are as many ways to God as there are people on earth. So this field guide is, above all, an *invitation to freely explore* with an open mind and heart, rather than laying out a set of rules and procedures to be followed.

Importantly, others have gone before us (including some who are widely recognised as spiritual authorities or masters) and they have left behind some very inspirational and helpful *maps* which we might choose to follow. Only a few of these are included in this guide, as well as references to some other resources which might be helpful tools in nourishing our Catholic faith (personally, in our families and communally). In selecting these, the challenging circumstances of the Gulf Savannah Parish (a small, widely dispersed and remote Catholic community) have been taken into account.

This book is organised into two main parts or sections: the first covering some essential aspects of Christian faith and beliefs while the second part presents some practical and proven ways through which the Living God, as revealed by Jesus, might be encountered day-to-day, not only in our churches but also in our homes, in our paddocks, in our gardens and so on.

The pivotal chapter linking these two parts is *Thy Kingdom Come*. Interestingly, this was the last chapter written, after reflecting for some time on a very uneasy feeling that something very important was missing. In that chapter, I hope to present an enduring vision and mission on which we can confidently anchor our Catholic spiritualities into eternity. This is the same vision and mission which

Jesus of Nazareth witnessed to with every fibre of his being, and in everything that he said and did. It's the original, untarnished version which might also challenge *us* with a potentially very different, much more liberating and inclusive understanding of *church* than what we may have grown up with.

So, based on these considerations, this book contains information, or suggested guidelines, for:

- venturing into the mystery of God, as revealed by Jesus,
- a basic understanding of the Kingdom of God vision which Jesus proclaimed,
- developing a genuine Catholic spirituality,
- practising the presence of God,
- prayer and meditation,
- entering into the spiritual gift of silence,
- *do-it-yourself* (DIY) liturgies for use at home,
- how to read and pray the Bible, and
- understanding the practical aspects of the Sacraments, including for emergencies in remote areas when there is no Priest, Deacon or Religious available.

How do I Use It?

This field guide is designed so that, if you wish (and have the time), you could read it through from cover to cover. Alternatively, you might just want to read the parts most relevant to your own needs or circumstances at any particular time. I would recommend that you read the chapters up to, and including, *Thy Kingdom Come,* together as they are closely interrelated. In addition, this book might be a useful resource for prayerful study together with your family or friends in a small group setting, using the questions as points of group reflection and discussion.

This photo was taken in the Bungle Bungles of Western Australia, an unknown tourist trying to capture a moment of 'enlightenment' between sheer walls of dark, conglomerate rock.

SOME BIG QUESTIONS

Introduction

Before heading into aspects of our Catholic faith, beliefs and practices, it seems important to start from what is very real and very tangible—our common humanity and the search for values and meaning which we each share with every other person who has ever lived, and will ever live, or at least, those that take time to stand back and reflect more deeply from time to time. All religions, including Christianity, have a profound and foundational interest in the human person and also say something important about the human condition.

'What are your 'Big Questions'?

This chapter, therefore, very briefly recognises and discusses some fundamental questions confronting every human being. It is in pondering these (and similar) *big questions* that will contribute to, and perhaps ultimately determine and shape the enduring direction and meaning of our lives, and what room (if any) we allow for someone, or something, many people refer to as *God*.

Why do I exist at all?

The ultimate question! Another way to put this is: what is the purpose or meaning of my life? None of us willed ourselves into existence, and today we find ourselves with about seven billion other human beings on what seems to be a lonely planet in a vast universe stretching away into incomprehensible distances measured by millions of light years. What is the purpose of it all, and consequently, what is the real meaning and value of my own life?

When did you last ask yourself: why am I here, alive on this earth?

What was your answer?

What might be the answer of the person/s most dear to you?

My Year 6 religion classes—mostly 11-12 year olds—can quite easily recognise that there is a fundamental choice to be made here. We either believe that our existence is pure chance and has no real purpose other than to live, or we believe that humanity (and creation) is not just a product of pure chance and that we are here for some ultimate reason or purpose.

Unfortunately, science cannot help us at all. Resolving this choice for ourselves is a matter of faith and not of science. Science by its very nature doesn't ask, because the scientific methods cannot answer, such fundamental *why* questions. Science excels in finding out *how* things happen or how things work. So, we have the Big Bang Theory (not the TV show!) and the Theory of Evolution to explain origins of the universe and of life i.e. *how* these might have come into being.

Then an intelligent Year 6 religion class would generally come up against the two foundational options which cannot be definitely resolved or decided with any certainty: *Why would the Big Bang happen, and thus what caused it?*, on the one hand, and, *How did God come to exist?*, on the other hand. These are quite obvious questions even for 12 year olds. Do you think these questions are answerable? Are they even valid questions, logically speaking?

Answering the question, *Why do I exist at all?*, in any manner which is satisfactory, must bring into focus matters of our personal faith and beliefs. In addition, the way we answer this question will shape our very lives. ***Do you agree?***

What then is a Christian response to the question of *Why do I exist at all?* Christians believe that there *is* a higher purpose for our lives, that we were created by a loving God and made in God's image (Genesis 1:27), and therefore set apart from any other created being or object. We were created to come to know and to love God, and to love one another in the school of love we call humanity, following the example and the witness of Jesus Christ.

Christians understand creation as an act of pure, unconditional love, pouring out from the very heart of God. Nevertheless, our participation in this Divine Love—which is freely extended to us to receive and then to share with others—is never coerced but always, and in all times, *invited*. We were each given free will which God has never, and will never, violate. The choice will always be ours.

> *Do you think these beliefs are reasonable or do they require Christians to abandon reason altogether? (More on this later.)*
>
> *Do you accept that you are more than just a physical body? If so, how do you look after your soul or spirit?*

Christians also believe that human beings are not just lumps of physical matter, bunches of atoms, molecules (stardust?) and neurons. Human beings are therefore never fully understandable nor ultimately predictable through scientific enquiry and investigation. No, we also believe that each person has a fathomless soul or spirit which makes each of us a unique, and thus a very special, human being. It is this soul that we believe is created *in God's image* and thus transcends our *material selves* in this life and in the one to come. Within the depths of each unique human soul, the depths of God may be encountered and probed.

Why is there suffering ... and death?

Some people at this stage would already be saying, *Well, okay, if there is a loving God, why is there so much suffering and evil in the world?* They will quite reasonably argue that, if God is all powerful, *Why isn't all suffering stopped?* or, *How can the loving God who you believe in allow so much suffering and seemingly allow evil to prosper?* Of course, the ultimate question in this vein is, *Why do I have to die?*

Whole books have already been written on the mystery of suffering and it would be the height of arrogance to even attempt to do this subject any justice or pretend that easy—or any—universally satisfying answers to these questions exist. So this discussion will necessarily be limited to a few, hopefully useful, observations and further questions for reflection by you, the reader.

Firstly, have you also found that suffering frequently evokes an extraordinary caring, compassionate and loving response which, without minimising in any way the hardship of the distress or pain being experienced, highlights the very, very best of humanity? Here in Ravenshoe we saw this very clearly after the terrible café explosion in 2015, not only in the immediate response of our own community but also in the incredible outpouring of generosity and concern for months afterwards from right across Australia for those affected. We also saw it with the mobilisation of the 'Mud Army' after the Brisbane floods, and again here in Ravenshoe, we have been privileged to both witness and channel the incredible support extended to our Community Drought Appeal in recent years for drought affected graziers in the neighbouring Gulf Savannah.

Secondly, if we ask, *Why the suffering?*, do you think we should also ask questions such as, *Why so much abundance and beauty in all of creation? Why are there so many colours and not just shades of grey? Why music,* and *Why humour? Why is there love and self-sacrifice, and so on?* Why only question the existence of suffering and not **balance** this out with questions about the reason for these life-giving and very positive elements of human existence?

Thirdly, can we really imagine how boring and bland life would be if there were no suffering? Would any of us know how good we had it and would our tendency towards arrogance and self-sufficiency have any bounds? Of course, Christians hope for a place where, *He will wipe every tear from their eyes. Death will be no more; mourning and crying and pain will be no more, for the first things have passed away* (Rev 21:4) ... but, perhaps thankfully, this place will not be found on earth.

Finally, the Christian faith accepts that suffering can also be transformative and redemptive, not because Christians are in some way masochists, but because Jesus transformed His own—and indeed all—suffering once and for all on Easter Sunday. It was an event so radical and profound that it turned the lives of His followers upside down and continues to do so today. Many have been prepared to die for their faith and confidence in this pivotal, world, and life-changing event.

In the same manner, Christians are required to confront, and never to accommodate, evil. We don't have to look very far to recognise that there is real and present evil in the world; evil is evident in the acts of individuals, groups, organisations and even nations. Terror is inflicted on unsuspecting civilians almost every week, often in the name of religion; the poor in developing countries are routinely exploited by multinationals so that others can wear the latest fashions sold at ridiculously exorbitant margins; domestic violence is endemic in our society; we have people selling drugs like ice to kids; and on and on this list grows.

> *Do you agree that there is a universal 'code of behaviour' for all humankind, irrespective of place or culture?*
>
> *If so, where might such a code have come from?*

As the saying goes, *All it takes for evil to triumph is for good people to do nothing.* Interestingly, one doesn't have to be a Christian to recognise the presence of evil and to challenge it; it seems that all humans and cultures are programmed with what seems to be a universal code of behaviour that recognises actions such as killing, stealing, oppression and the like are wrong. Nevertheless, confronting evil is usually risky and requires courage as well as a preparedness to step out of one's secure comfort zone.

Are we surprised therefore that Jesus challenges His followers to find their redemption and fullness of life **in taking up their crosses?** *If any want to become my followers, let them deny themselves and take up their cross daily and follow me. For those who want to save their life will lose it, and those who lose their life for my sake will save it. (Luke 9: 23-24)* Isn't that an interesting counter-cultural message for today?

But he also said, *Come to me, all you that are weary and are carrying heavy burdens and I will give you rest* (Matthew 11:28)

> You might like to reflect on a time in your life when you experienced great suffering.
>
> What helped to carry you through and how were you changed by the experience?

So, Christians following in the footsteps of Jesus cannot and should not expect a life that is devoid of all suffering, or a life that can validly remain indifferent to the evil that exists around us. Jesus didn't live such a life and nor will we. *When suffering comes our way, as it must, we trust in faith that God will see us through; that the suffering we experience never has the last and final word, and cannot, therefore, ever define us.*

Easter Sunday follows Good Friday; when all seemed lost, it was all only really just beginning!

Can faith also be reasonable?

The short answer to this question is that it has to be; at the least faith and reason should not be opposed to one another or be mutually exclusive. A mature and balanced faith doesn't abandon reason and is also open to critical and respectful dialogue and inquiry if it is to be credible in the marketplace of ideas. By way of contrast, some public 'discussions' of matters of faith and religion unfortunately involve fundamentalists—people on both sides who are unable to really listen to other viewpoints and also resort to ridicule and insult to protect their positions and views.

To illustrate this, on the one hand, there are Christian fundamentalists who firmly believe that the Bible is historically factual from cover to cover, and thus the world can only be several thousand years old. Consequently, they disbelieve and ignore all the scientific evidence to the contrary. Some would describe this as faith abandoning reason. On the other hand, there are also atheist scientists who (sometimes quite aggressively) believe that everything is ultimately explicable through matter, the rules of nature or physics, and by scientific observation. They thus have their own creed which can also come across as just as fundamentalist; there is no place for any god, or any mystery that cannot ultimately be explained using reason alone. Reason thus abandons any faith ... and wisdom.

Neither extreme is at all helpful and often seems to give rise to what might be described as a *clash of ignorance*. For Christians, faith and reason should work in harmony, especially given that our capacity to think, question and work things out are all God's gifts in the first place.

So what are some of the factors that suggest that Christian faith is reasonable? Potentially a number of lists might be produced, but here is one offered for consideration and evaluation by you, the reader:

- There is an awesome scale, complexity, diversity and beauty evident within creation which some refer to as God's first book of revelation.
- For all its knowledge and skills, science is unable to create life in even the smallest of, say, grass seeds. Science can only manipulate what already has the life-force within, yet we can see—if we wish to—an amazing diversity of life. Could this possibly have happened completely at random, a result of unintended chance?
- There is an alignment of many people, places and times referred to in the Bible with the discoveries of modern archaeology.

- The existence of a Jesus of Nazareth, His baptism in the Jordan by John the Baptist, and execution on a cross in the time of Pontius Pilate, are not disputed by most scholars as being historical facts.

- There is strong Biblical evidence that Jesus' disciples were transformed through their belief that Jesus had indeed risen on that first Easter Sunday; from a rather dull, ignorant and frightened group they became fearless evangelists, prepared to die for their belief in Jesus the Christ. It is believed that all the Apostles except John were martyred and many have been martyred for their Christian belief since that time.

- The Church can trace its origins through written records (separate to the Bible) into the first decades of the existence of Christianity.

- Despite all its faults—and the terrible evils the church has committed over the centuries—the Christian faith has profoundly shaped and positively influenced entire cultures and societies, influences which continue into the present day; hospitals and schools, accessible to all, were firstly Christian undertakings. So many people living lives shaped by Christian values have had profoundly positive influences on their families, communities, or societies.

- Many Christians have personally experienced things and events that simply cannot be explained outside of belief in God; these include unexpected answers to prayers, and unsought revelations welling up from, *I know not where* within.

- Christians have not been able to find a better compass for their lives which gives an enduring meaning and purpose, then to love God and to love their neighbour.

After reading this list, is there anything you disagree with, or would want to add?

How do I Become a Christian or a Catholic?

This is a very good question! From one perspective, the answer seems simple—becoming a Christian or Catholic is tied to the moment when a person is baptised (christened), either as a baby, or after suitable preparation, as an older child or adult. However, the event of being baptised might be compared to signing on to a sporting club to play with a team. After the signing on, we then learn how to *play the game*, through training, practice, and then striving for excellence as a player. Hopefully this will all be under the guidance of a caring coach who both inspires and challenges. Even the best sportsmen and women— those who are publicly recognised and celebrated—would never say that they had achieved perfection, knowing full well that one untimely error can have big consequences for them and for their team e.g. the loss of a premiership.

Becoming a Christian or Catholic follows a similar pattern. Being baptised or christened is really like a signing on to a team; yes, a very different sort of team but nevertheless needing the same sort of ongoing commitment to learn, to train and to practice, in order to become a disciple of Jesus. This process of becoming is a lifelong journey which, for most people, will include many ups and downs, unexpected twists and turns, times of doubt and darkness, and moments of sheer joy with a felt sense of God's real presence and grace.

In my own case, I was baptised shortly after I was born in June 1952 and now, at 67 years of age, I am very much aware that I am still *becoming* a Catholic. I think I have made some progress as a disciple of Jesus ... but there is still a long way to go, and that's okay!

Have *you* been feeling some stirring or questioning deep within, perhaps even a sense of a nameless Presence of someone, or something, active in your life, or in the unique circumstances of the world in which you live every day? Or perhaps you feel that things just haven't been working out for you—perhaps your life has become an unhappy mess where it is difficult to find lasting meaning, or even hope? If these, or similar situations apply to you, then it could well be that they are actually invitations to change: perhaps calls to sign-on, or re-commit, to a team where everyone is welcome no matter who or what you are, where everyone is equal, where everyone is loved unconditionally ... without exception.

Is it time for a change? If it is, then you might like to consider a simple, heartfelt prayer, perhaps something like this:

> Jesus, I don't know much about you, or if you are even there, or listening to me, but I need help please. I really want to live my life in a deeper and more meaningful way, and to become a better and more loving person. For my part, and from this moment, I commit myself to you and humbly ask for your help in becoming your disciple. Please reveal yourself to me, help me to learn about you and to follow your example and teachings. Amen.

Yes, I know that saying this prayer can feel like stepping off a cliff while blindfolded! Some people can also worry about the cost of such a commitment, and what seems to be a loss of personal freedom in following Jesus' way of being fully alive, a way which also has obligations and expectations. I have had those worries myself, but now, I don't think I have ever felt freer than I have in being a Christian.

I also know from personal experience—and from the testimonies of others—that this quote from scripture is absolutely true:

> Ask, and it will be given to you; search, and you will find; knock, and the door will be opened for you. For everyone who asks receives, and everyone who searches finds, and for everyone who knocks, the door will be opened. Is there anyone among you who, if your child asks for bread, will give a stone? Or if the child asks for a fish, will give a snake? If you then, who are evil, know how to give good gifts to your children, how much more will your Father in heaven give good things to those who ask him! (Matthew 7:7-11)

So dear reader, if this brief section or something else in this field guide has inspired you to **become** a Catholic or Christian, and you have made a first step by saying a prayer such as the above, then the next step is to find a person who can be your spiritual mentor or guide, and hopefully, a supportive church community. Ask your friends or contact a Priest, Deacon or Religious, or this author.

Summary

As stated at the start of this chapter, as thinking human beings we are challenged to navigate through some very big questions which go to the very heart of the nature and purpose of our existence. These are timeless questions anchored in our very humanity. In probing and pondering them, many (but not all) come to a position of faith in a God as the source of all creation and thus discard the alternative of there being no ultimate meaning to existence or to human suffering, or to death. For these people, developing a life of faith does not require that reason be abandoned, or minds be *switched off*. No, on the contrary, we are required to use everything that is at our disposal. In the words of Jesus, *You shall love the Lord your God with all your heart, and with all your soul, and with **all your mind**. This is the greatest and first commandment.* (Matthew 22:37-38)

Living this commandment is a life-long journey of **becoming** Christian or Catholic, and the very first step can be as simple as a short, but heartfelt prayer, reaching out to God asking for help.

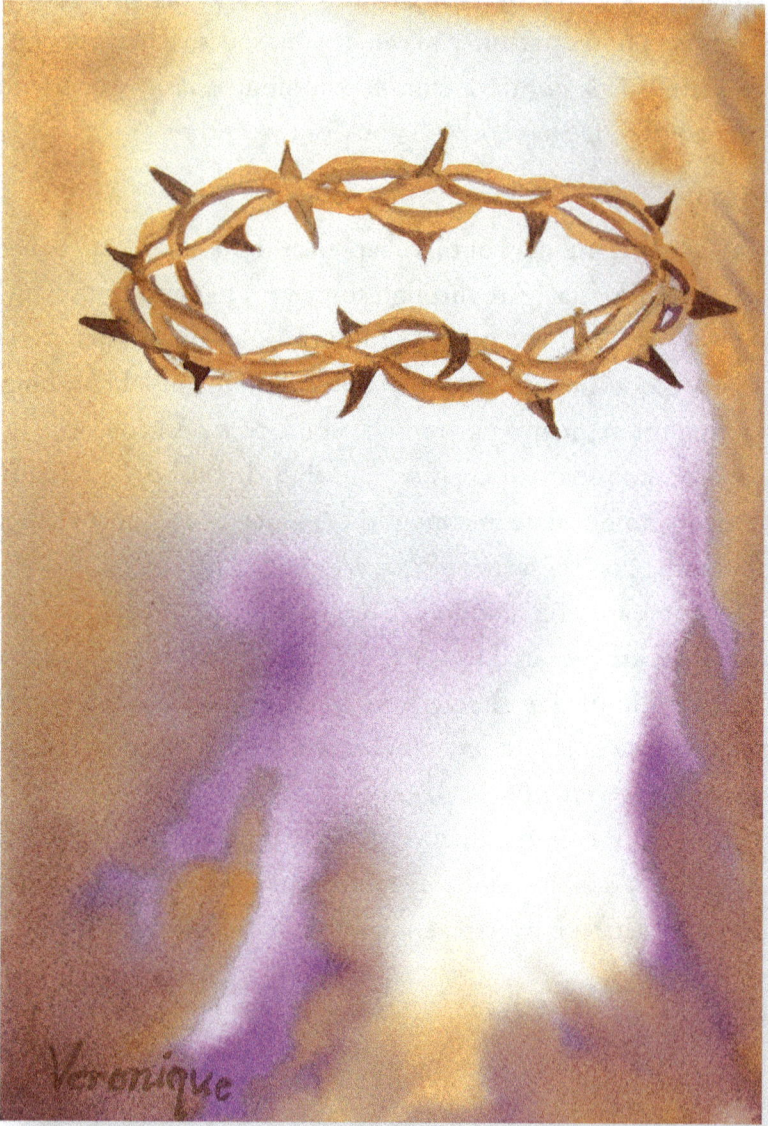

An intuitive painting, reminding us that the Christian revelation of God is as One who suffers for us and with us, but that beyond any suffering lies the light and hope of Eternal Life

What is God Really Like?

Overview

Having considered some big questions arising from our very humanity, and either confirming or perhaps really admitting for the first time, that God is indeed a possibility, we might then find ourselves asking, *What would this God be like?*

If deciding what to include (or not) in this field guide about being Catholic isn't challenging enough, fully or completely answering this question is, of course, totally impossible. Indeed, some wise person once said that if we added up all the experiences and insights and all the books ever written, the total of all this is still *complete darkness* in terms of understanding who God is in and of Godself (yes, this is an unusual word, but it avoids giving God a gender as we would do by using *Himself*). And yet, we must try (and we can) penetrate some way into this darkness in order to have anything meaningful to say at all. So that is what this brief chapter will attempt to do, to provide a very brief thumbnail sketch of some important aspects of the Christian understanding of God.

Some Images of God

However, let's firstly consider some possible images that we may have of God, the god/s that we (or others) have created or have become comfortable with—rather than who God actually is. You might find yourself having similar created images or understandings.

> *Please spend a moment reflecting on what image (if any) you have of God?*
>
> *Which of these (or other) lesser gods might have been presented to you in what you were taught or experienced earlier in life?*

- **Santa Claus:** This god (notice the 'g' is not capitalised to reflect that this is a humanly created god) is like a kindly old man who we can ask for things ... but only if we are on his *nice* list.
- **Superman:** We call for help to this god only when we are in trouble and when he has fixed our problems we expect him to fly off, as it were, out of our lives and consciousness ... until the next time we call for help.
- **Asleep in the sky ... somewhere:** This god is a long, long way away and doesn't seem to be very interested in me at all.
- **Myth:** Just like the ancient gods and goddesses of ancient Rome and Greece, any god is just a myth, a made up story, and consequently any religion could only be *opium of the people* (Karl Marx).
- **An Angry Judge:** This god is like a cosmic tyrant, waiting to *zap* and punish anyone who misbehaves, leaving people wondering if they will ever be good enough to be acceptable (many older Catholics might well have such an image of god given an emphasis in their religious upbringing as children on sin and on being *good* in order to earn this god's love).

In truth, it seems quite likely that these images (or shadows of them) are involved in our personal relationships with God to a greater or lesser extent at various stages of our lives, and in the changing circumstances in which we find ourselves. For example, most of us have probably experienced attempts at prayer to be like 'talking into empty space', or to a god who is fast asleep in some far distant galaxy.

So, aware of these *lesser gods*, let us now highlight aspects of the Christian understanding and experience of God, revealed to us especially in and through *Jesus, the Christ, the ultimate and unsurpassable image of God.*

Jesus the Christ

Once again, entire libraries have been written on Jesus so this chapter can only provide the briefest of thumbnail sketches. At the outset, it is important that to note that *Christ* was not the surname of Jesus but instead means *Messiah, Anointed One* or *Saviour*. It was only after His resurrection that Jesus was referred to as the Christ.

> *Before reading too much further, you might like to bring to mind some things you already know about Jesus.*
>
> *'But who do you say that I am?' (Luke 9:20)*

Jesus of Nazareth was born sometime in the period 6-4 BC, although scholars have not been able to determine a precise date. Similarly, we do not have a precise date for his death by crucifixion, but scholars generally agree it was sometime between the years 30-33 AD. What is not seriously questioned anymore as a historical fact is that there *was* a man known as Jesus of Nazareth who was also the founder of Christianity. Both Biblical and independent (or non-Biblical) sources testify to this. For example, one of these was Josephus Ben Matthias, a Jewish historian whose writings late in the first century, refer to Jesus, Jesus' brother James, and Pilate, the Roman Governor who condemned Jesus to death.

According to the four separate Gospel accounts—or *portraits*—of Jesus, He was raised in a family of devout Jews, fulfilling all the requirements of the Jewish religion. During His childhood, adolescence and early adulthood, He lived a humble and hidden life in a little rural village as a carpenter's son, possibly becoming a carpenter Himself. At about the age of 30, He entered the public arena and, very dramatically, through the witness of His entire being and his ministry (especially to the poor, the sick and the outcasts of Jewish society) set about proclaiming the Kingdom of God; a kingdom of love, peace and justice for all, where the poor and disadvantaged have priority and a kingdom where, *the last will be first and the first will be last* (Matthew 20:16). (There will be more on the centrality of the Kingdom of God for Christianity in the Chapter: *Thy Kingdom Come.*)

This proclamation was something radically new; nowhere in the Hebrew Scriptures (or Old Testament) is there any reference to *the Kingdom of God*. In a nutshell, Jesus proclaimed—both in the Jewish synagogues and throughout the countryside—an entirely new revelation of the nature of God and what being in relationship with God should look like. He challenged the premise that simply following the letter of the Jewish religious laws was enough to be acceptable to God. By way of stark contrast, the currency of the Kingdom that Jesus proclaimed is *love*.

It was because Jesus and His message were so radical but so *real* and so *attractive*, that He gained a huge following which then became a threat to both the religious and political authorities at that time. Consequently, He encountered increasing levels of hostility and opposition as he became more and more popular. This eventually led to His arrest, condemnation and execution as a common criminal by crucifixion; a horrific death which nevertheless bequeathed the Cross as the enduring symbol of God's great love for humankind.

Despite this hostility and opposition, Jesus gathered around him a small group of disciples who stayed with Him; following Him along many dusty tracks as Jesus proclaimed the Good News. They were a rather motley and ordinary lot, both men and women. Whilst Jesus spent a great deal of time with them, teaching through His words and actions, most of them did not really understand who Jesus really was and what He was on about. That understanding was to come later.

And yet, it was this same group of ordinary people, just like you and I, who had come to love Jesus so much that they surrendered their lives to His will, in many cases leaving their old lives behind. *What was it about Him that was so attractive?*

After Jesus died on the cross and was buried, this same group of people became so convinced that Jesus had been resurrected on that first Easter Sunday, that they were prepared to die for this belief, and many of them did. They came to believe that Jesus was the Christ or Messiah who had been promised through the Jewish prophets. From being a somewhat dull and fearful bunch of disciples, hiding away after Jesus was crucified, they were transformed into the fearless evangelists on whom the Catholic Church was built ... and here you are today, reading this nearly 2000 years later.

Through many generations, back to the time of Christ, the Good News has been handed down from person to person.

Like those first disciples, we are each invited to also enter into life-changing relationships with Jesus the Christ, as the Son of God. It won't be an easy life being a Christian—Jesus certainly didn't have an easy time of it—but if you are searching for a life that can be dripping with meaning, purpose and unconditional, eternal love, then this is what being a disciple of Jesus the Christ offers.

> *What gives your life real and lasting purpose and meaning now?*
>
> *Do you think your answer will be the same in the future?*

Christian Revelation of God

Let us then examine some of the most important elements of the Christian revelation of God, the God whom Jesus revealed. These are:

God is Trinity, Father, Son and Holy Spirit and yet One God. Whenever we Catholics (or Christians) don't really understand from human experience how something can be, we call it a *mystery*, and understanding God as *Three Yet One*, is the mystery of mysteries. Yet, the New Testament tells us very clearly that Jesus always spoke and preached about His Father ... but never preached about Himself. The Holy Spirit, who was sent down on the unsuspecting disciples at the first Pentecost, always points people to Jesus, the Son of God, seeking to bring everyone into a closer relationship with both the Son and the Father.

> *What difference, if any, does it make to you that the Christian experience and understanding of God is as Trinity, a relationship of infinite love between Father, Son and Spirit?*

In the actions and witness of the members of the Trinity, Christians have, over many centuries, come to understand God as a God in infinitely loving relationships **within**, between Father, Son and Spirit as a Trinity, each focussed on the other—the real meaning of love even as we humans understand it. The God who Jesus revealed is, therefore, not some lonely deity far away, somewhere out there in splendid isolation up in the heavens, but a God as Trinity, a Trinity of love overflowing as the very source and sustaining life of *all* creation. It is into this creation that Jesus, the Word of God was sent and became for all time *God with us*, the meaning of *Emmanuel*.

A God of Unconditional Love – A Love that is Our Birthright and Can Never be Earnt.

Please permit me to share a little personal testimony to illustrate the importance of really understanding this statement ...

> *Do you really believe that there is nothing that you could ever do that will separate you from God's unconditional love, and God's readiness to forgive?*

Even though I went to Catholic schools for most of my young life, it wasn't until I was 34 years old and after some serious drifting in matters of faith, that my heart was opened to this truth, and it has made all the difference. I used to think that I *first* had to be perfect in order to be acceptable to God and to be loved by God. This, I think, was the same lesson a lot of Catholics of my generation learnt as children and, you know what, it is completely and utterly *wrong!*

The First Letter of John in the New Testament makes this very clear, *In this is love, not that we loved God but that he loved us and sent his Son to be the atoning sacrifice for our sins* (I John 4: 10). In other words, God loved us *first*, from the time even before we were born, certainly well before we became aware of God and our birthright as Christians. *For it was you who formed my inward parts; you knit me together in my mother's womb* (Psalm 139:13).

Jesus gave a wonderful illustration of this unchanging and unconditional love of God in his parable of the Prodigal Son in the Gospel of Luke (15: 11-32). In this story we learn about a younger son who essentially trashes his inheritance and his relationship with his father, opting for a life of self-indulgence and wastefulness. When he is destitute and comes to his senses, he then heads for home with an apology prepared for his 'old man'. The father who has clearly been watching and waiting for him to come back home, madly rushes to meet him with open arms and then throws a big party because his son, ... *was dead and has come to life; he was lost and has been found* (Luke 15:32).

For many Christians—this one included—this is a favourite image of God, that of a father running with open arms to meet a child who has decided to return home. Do you relate to this image as well? Rather than sitting back and watching us stumble around, the God whom Jesus revealed is like our life-partner or coach, wanting— no, deeply yearning—for us to succeed.

God loves us into life, so that we can *become* the people that we were created to be!

God is Very Close. *Indeed he is not far from each one of us; for in him we live and move and have our being* (Acts 17:27-28). Recently I read this little story which speaks about the closeness of God. I found it very thought provoking and I hope you will too.

> 'How does a person seek union with God?', the seeker asked.
> 'The harder you seek,' the teacher said, 'the more distance you create between God and you.'
> 'So what does one do about the distance?'
> 'Understand that it isn't there' the teacher said.
> 'Does that mean that God and I are one?', the seeker said.
> 'Not one. Not two.'
> 'How is that possible?', the seeker asked.
> 'The sun and its light, the ocean and the wave, the singer and the song. Not one. Not two.'[4]

God's presence is always probing our souls and is *within us* to be realized, not outside of us to be stumbled upon. He certainly doesn't

---

4   Quoted in Chittister, J OSB. (1992) *The Rule of Benedict: Insights for the Ages.* New York: Crossroad. P64

only come as a passenger in Father's, Sister's or the Deacon's car, or is in any way restricted to just being present in our church buildings!

Know Jesus, Know God. If we really want to know God, then we need to get to know Jesus the Christ: through prayer, through immersing ourselves in the Gospel stories, and participation in the Mass and the Sacraments whenever we can. Jesus yearns for each one of us to know Him more fully, and to enter into a unique and very personal relationship with us. However, Jesus will never trespass into our souls against our free wills when He is not wanted. Rather we might each hear him saying, *Listen! I am standing at the door, knocking; if you hear my voice and open the door, I will come in to you and eat with you, and you with me* (Rev 3:20). He never gives up or grows tired of knocking on the doors of our souls, hoping that we will open them for Him.

God's Spirit is Wild and Free. Just as the disciples found out on the first Pentecost, occasionally God's Spirit just comes upon us when we least expect it, and in ways that we could not possibly have imagined. Sometimes when this occurs, our lives are also fundamentally changed. Other times are less dramatic but we might then receive a profound or inspired new insight, from *we know not where*, into a situation or a problem which has been troubling us, but clearly an insight we ourselves did not think, or will, into existence.

Jesus, although raised as a devout Jew, subsequently exercised a public ministry that could only be considered *wild and free*; roundly challenging the established order, rules and practices of both His religion and His culture. It was this challenge that the religious and political authorities just couldn't handle or allow. From His Father's perspective, however, Jesus' public life and ministry was anything but wild and free in that Jesus was completely devoted to obeying His Father's will to inaugurate and proclaim the Kingdom of God.

Veronique

'Now the Lord is the Spirit, and where the Spirit of the Lord is, there is freedom.'
(2 Corinthians 3:17)

We can run into big trouble when we overlook that God's very nature is unable to be mustered or contained in any way. Sometimes Christian churches have been presumptuous, and actually diminish what God has revealed, in claiming that their way is the only way in which people can fully encounter God. Wars have come from this.

Similarly, at a personal level, we can also try to contain and tame God, for example, by clutching onto cherished devotional and liturgical practices, and rules with which we have become very comfortable and are afraid to change for any reason. Perhaps we can only really become alive as Catholics (or Christians) when we allow ourselves to share in some of God's wildness and freedom?

Beware of *Going it Alone.* If we accept the fact that God is just too big for anybody or for everybody to comprehend, then the risks for any of us

> *A 'do it yourself' Christianity is an impossibility! Do you agree or disagree, and why?*

in just *going it alone*, with our own personal and private search for God, should be very obvious. Yet many people seem to be trying to do just that. I am reminded of the saying, *an isolated Christian is a paralysed Christian*

If we do try to go it alone, we can so easily deceive ourselves (cults have come from this) and we miss out on the experiences and insights of others which can amplify and affirm our own spiritual journeys. There is a very rich treasure left behind by those who have gone before us: the exemplary witness and lives of the Saints, great spiritual writings from recognised spiritual masters (starting from the very first centuries of Christianity), guidance for various types of prayer to suit different personalities, art and music to lift our souls and a variety of liturgies to achieve the same ... the list goes on. We don't have to—and shouldn't even try— to *reinvent the wheel* for ourselves.

From the outset, Christianity has been a faith in which any revelation of God is shared and tested within a community of believers. Of course, this poses special—but not insurmountable—challenges for those living in isolated circumstances out in the bush, but more on this in a later chapter.

Summary

This chapter has painted what might best be referred to as a thumbnail sketch of the Christian understanding of God, as revealed by and through Jesus the Christ, Son of God, who entered the world stage some 2000 years ago and revealed God as a Trinity of Father, Son and Spirit, a God of unconditional and infinite love.

It is this great love that is offered (but never forced) for every human being to freely receive and accept, and in so doing to be loved into life by our Creator, to become the people that we are meant to be—fully human, fully alive. Such love can never be earned through any merit on our part, by *being good*; no, it's our very birthright which can never be taken from us.

The time is fulfilled, and the kingdom of God has come near; repent, and believe in the good news. (Mark 1:15)

'THY KINGDOM COME'

Introduction

Thy Kingdom Come is, for most Catholics, a very familiar line in the Lord's Prayer; the prayer which Jesus Himself taught His disciples when they asked Him to teach them how to pray. Many of us can probably pray this prayer without thinking, by rote, and yet within these three words lays one of the most important keys to our Christian faith and how it is perceived and lived. As suggested in the introduction, this chapter is pivotal for this book; an essential bridge between the basic elements of Catholic faith and beliefs covered in the preceding chapters and the practice of that faith in a way that is consistent with what Jesus proclaimed.

Before reading on, what do you understand by the phrase Kingdom of God?

Above all, it is my hope that this chapter will suggest—or perhaps remind you of—some very important insights into the original and unalterable message or Good News of Jesus, namely His proclamation of the Kingdom of God. In engaging with, and prayerfully reflecting on, this original message, perhaps each of us might better discern how we can cooperate with God's Spirit in building this Kingdom in our own unique circumstances, irrespective of where we live or how distant we feel—whether spiritually or geographically—from the Church.

What is the Kingdom of God?

First and foremost, the Kingdom of God proclaimed by Jesus is *not* the same as the Catholic Church, or any Christian church, or indeed even the sum of all these churches considered together. It is infinitely greater in vision, scope and mission than the geographical, spiritual and other boundaries that define any or all churches.

The goal of Jesus' life and ministry was to proclaim and witness to the Kingdom of God, to announce its arrival in His person and to reveal its values in everything that He said and did. Jesus did not proclaim Himself... nor did He emphasize the arrival of a new church. In the Gospel accounts, Jesus refers to the Kingdom or Reign of God about 67 times, but the word church is mentioned only four times!

In which parts of your life do you feel God's Spirit is in control?

How has the Kingdom of God penetrated our world to make it a better place?

The Kingdom of God can be understood as the universal stage for the movement of God's wild and free Spirit, able to *break through* in all places and in all times. Kirk describes living in this Kingdom as, ... *life free from the reign of all those forces that enslave humanity ... the sphere of life where God's spirit is in control.*[5] Fuellenbach emphasizes that the Kingdom of God is not, *just purely spiritual or outside of this world, [but refers to:], a total, global, and structural transfiguration and revolution of the reality of all human beings; it means the cosmos purified of all evils and full of the reality of God.*[6] He also emphasizes the **freedom** that characterises membership of the

---

5   A.J. Kirk, What is Mission? Theological Explorations (Minneapolis: Fortress Press, 2000), 29

6   John Fuellenbach, *The Kingdom of God: The Message of Jesus Today*, 96

Kingdom, *freedom* to respond to God's creative love and to cooperate with the coming of the Kingdom.

To delve into this further, Jesus proclaimed and gave witness to a Kingdom of God vision and mission that is:

- characterized by *love* (God's overflowing and unconditional love for us and all that is asked of us in return to show that we have really received this love, is that we strive to love God and to love one another – the Greatest Commandment),
- marked by *joy* (a deep joy in being loved unconditionally just for who we are; this joy being very different to the pursuit of happiness),
- continually refreshed and renewed by the *firm hope* of the final triumph of God's reign (that in the end—no matter what is happening now or might happen in future—God will have *the last word* and trusting that, *all things work together for good for those who love God, who are called according to his purpose* (Romans 8: 28),
- integrated and not capable of being sub-divided into *sacred* and *secular* (especially any notions that humanity is somehow divided, with those that are *good* and thus *saved* being limited only to those lucky enough to be Christian; indeed a key Vatican II document *Gaudium et Spes* states that, *the Holy Spirit in ways known only to God offers all peoples ways of participating in the Paschal Mystery* (i.e. the death and resurrection of Jesus) (GS22)),
- able to be experienced now through God's Spirit (needing the assistance of the Spirit to discern where the Kingdom is *breaking through* in the concrete circumstances of our own lives, in our families and communities),
- always showing an *authentic, preferential option for the poor and disadvantaged* (just as Jesus did in ministering to the sick and outcasts of his time),
- embracing work for *justice and peace, and concern for the environment* (as valid signs of the reign of God), and,

- able to be present within each individual, as well as within organizations, societies and cultures (that the Kingdom frontiers can be discovered in the *hearts* of each of these entities).

> *To what extent are these values of the Kingdom of God, as revealed by Jesus, visible in your life, the life of your family, your community or parish, the broader Church?*
>
> *Why not take a few minutes to reflect on where God's Spirit might be moving in your own life or circumstances right now, where the Kingdom of God might be breaking through to change something or someone, or perhaps to change you?*

The Kingdom of God and the Church

The importance and pre-eminence of the Kingdom of God was highlighted by Pope Paul VI, *As an evangelizer, Christ first of all proclaims a kingdom, the kingdom of God; and this is so important that, by comparison, everything else becomes the rest, which is 'given in addition'. Only the kingdom therefore is absolute, and it makes everything else relative.*[7]

> *Before proceeding, please stop for a moment and think about the word 'church'. What does this mean or signify for you?*
>
> *Did you immediately think of a building?*

Significantly, the Church is included among *the rest*. However, this does not in any way diminish its importance because—when at its best—the Church makes Christ present and real as a sacrament (understood as a sign and instrument) both of a very closely knit union with God and of the unity of all people[8]. In other words,

---

7   Pope Paul VI, *On Evangelization in the Modern World (Evangelii Nuntiandi)*, 15, 8 Dec 75; http://www.vatican.va/holy_father/paul_vi/apost_exhortations/documents/hf_p-vi_exh_19751208_evangelii-nuntiandi_en.html, (4Apr 09), 8

8   From *Evangelii Gaudium (Joy of the Gospel)* by Pope Francis: "The Church is sent by Jesus Christ as the sacrament of the salvation offered by God" (EG 102)

the Church should give *flesh and blood* to the ongoing presence and action of God in the world, including through the witness and actions of those who call themselves Christian. In this sense, while we might have been conditioned to think of a building when we see or hear the word *church*, it is better and more accurately understood to be an assembly of people all united in faith in Jesus the Christ striving to live the Gospel that He preached and witnessed to.

Fuellenbach describes the Church as a *Kingdom colony*[9] to witness to the reality of the Kingdom present today,

> *How do you feel about this paragraph which subordinates the Church to the Kingdom of God?*

while pointing the way to its future fulfillment. This is very, very important: ***the Church's mission and very reason for its existence is to give flesh to the reality of the Kingdom, to be a credible witness to this same Kingdom in every place and time.*** Clearly it doesn't always do this very well; in the past, the Catholic Church tended to equate itself to the Kingdom of God and this brought with it a range of unwelcome distortions of the Good News of Christ: a sense of triumphalism, inability to admit mistakes and the like. Some might argue that little has changed and that the Church is still far too concerned about preserving itself rather than furthering its core mission and purpose in proclaiming the Kingdom of God.

So it seems that two things are needed: to give priority to proclaiming and building the Kingdom of God in our local circumstances and situations while, at the same time, (re)forming our Parishes, Diocese and the global Church into more credible witnesses for this Kingdom, clearly displaying to a spiritually hungry world some of the key elements of the Kingdom of God vision and mission as outlined above. Surely the Church is most *being church*—at each and every level—when it is serving the Kingdom and not itself.

---

9   John Fuellenbach, *The Kingdom of God: The Message of Jesus Today*, 15

A Kingdom Vision and Mission

Each of us could, of course, just wait for the Church to act. Where does that leave us, however, if the pace of change is too slow, or if we already feel cut off and alienated, or if the Church as an institution just continues with *business as usual*, seeking firstly to preserve itself and its ways of doing things, especially its clerical power and control structures, rather than seeking *first the Kingdom of God and His righteousness* (Matt 6:33)?

I have personally struggled with these matters, especially in the discernment journey leading to my ordination. How could I commit myself to such a flawed and imperfect institution? Is the Church's vision and understanding of its mission sufficiently clear, or has it become too distorted and overlaid with second-order *stuff* over the past 2,000 years? It was then that I was exposed to the very rich theology of the Kingdom of God and its intimate connection to the nature of God as revealed by Jesus. In this ***original vision and proclamation of Jesus***, we are able to find:

- an overarching vision providing an explanation of the purpose and meaning of our existence,
- a mission-oriented, life goal to live for, work for and if needed, to die for, a goal that extends well beyond simply working for the maintenance of the Church in and of itself,
- a fraternity potentially open to all, whether in the Church or not, and,
- a mission imbued with faith, hope and love, always reaching out to others.

It was as if a bright light had turned on inside the deepest part of me ... an *aha* moment ... a higher call that seemed as if it would sustain me for the rest of my life. Of course, since then, the practical day-to-day issues and concerns of being a Permanent Deacon within the Church have sometimes pushed this clarity of vision and purpose into the background, even threatening to hide it altogether. However, in quieter moments and especially in writing this, Jesus' Kingdom of God vision and mission seems as fresh and as life-giving as when I first encountered it more than a decade ago.

More importantly, with God's grace, each of us can make the Kingdom of God real and present for others. However, individually, we can never be *church*.

A Family is a Church?

On the other hand, can a family be a church? Yes, very much so. A Christian family can make the Kingdom of God very real and present for its members and, just as importantly, real and present for others connected to the family. In doing so, they make the *Church present and operative in those places and circumstances where only through them can it become the salt of the earth.*[10] This means that an isolated Catholic family on a cattle station—or indeed any family anywhere—is in fact a church when it strives to live and witness to the values of the Kingdom of God that Jesus proclaimed.

In my pastoral visits, I see so many families doing this, though probably not aware that they are, in fact, proclaiming the Kingdom of God through their words and actions. I have been very privileged to witness: great faithfulness to prayer, wonderful acts of kindness, and of real sacrificial love when others are in need. I've seen the loving day-to-day care of children and of those who are old and frail, the celebrations and joy of marking significant occasions, providing help for neighbours—sometimes hours away on dusty tracks—to *chase cattle*, and so on. These are all examples of how the core values of the Kingdom of God are being lived every day.

The Church also teaches that parents are always the first teachers of their children in the Catholic faith, and, in that sense, they are the ministers of their own little church! This doesn't require any sort of

---

10 Adapted from *Lumen Gentium*, 33

theology degree or training in ministry, but does require a deeply held desire to pass on this precious gift of faith than has been handed down to us through so many generations. There are plenty of resources available to help you ... just ask your Priest, Deacon or Religious!

> *My family is a church!*
>
> *Do you agree?*
>
> *If so, what might that mean for the practice of your Catholic faith?*
>
> *If you don't agree, how would you argue this?*

So, for those in the outback, rather than perhaps only thinking of *church* when Father, Sister or the Deacon is next in the nearest town for a service, possibly weeks or months away, is there perhaps a need for a complete change in this thinking? Alternatively, if we have tended to associate our understanding of *church* with the church building and Sunday Mass available just around the corner in a town or city, might there be a new way of understanding *church* as something much closer and more personal, as our own family, perhaps gathered around the kitchen table?

Of course, none of this means that each little family should be an independent little church with its own unique beliefs and practices. To be part of the church which Christ established, to be part of His family, means that each family should remain connected (or in communion) in some way with the broader Church and be willing to be guided by its beliefs and teachings. To do otherwise would be to become a sect or a cult, and there are real potential dangers in this, such as being led completely astray into practices and beliefs that are sometimes based on the establishment and maintenance of power and control, rather than on the Gospel of Jesus.

Summary

My sincere and heartfelt hope in writing this Chapter is that it has connected you, the reader, to a far bigger picture and vision on which to confidently and sustainably base your own Catholic faith, beliefs and practices. While not suggesting for a moment that the Church has no role here, I do think that we all must try to look through and beyond the Church to the greater reality and presence of the Kingdom of God which Jesus proclaimed and inaugurated. As has been suggested, our Church is but an agent representing and pointing to this infinitely bigger reality; the universal stage of God's movement and presence, referred to as the Kingdom of God. This is what Jesus came to reveal, this is what He lived and died for, and it is to full participation as members of this Kingdom to which *everyone* is invited.

On a much smaller and localized scale, I have briefly discussed the important role of a family as a church. Although at a micro-level of what it means to be church, Catholic families can nevertheless make the Kingdom of God very real and very present in their own unique circumstances. Indeed, where there is no other *show in town*, it is very important that they do so to witness to the real presence of this Kingdom for others, and thus help to build it up in our sometimes very troubled world.

My prayer in writing this Chapter is that God's Spirit will bring this Kingdom alive (or more alive) in each of our souls and then inspire us to commit ourselves to cooperate with God's Spirit to make this Kingdom real and present wherever, and whenever, we find ourselves. This could make each of us full participants in realizing that simple but very profound prayer, *Thy Kingdom Come*.

When you next pray the Lord's Prayer, why not ask where God's Spirit is inviting you to help His Kingdom to come ... it could be as simple as an act of kindness for someone, a change of heart or an act of forgiveness for a hurt!

An intuitive painting, suggesting spirituality as being without precise or definitive forms or structures.

CATHOLIC SPIRITUALITY

Overview

Oh, I believe in God alright, but I don't go to church.

Have you ever heard anyone say this? I have—many times.

Perhaps of the 90% or so of Catholics in Australia who do not participate in the sacramental or liturgical life of the church regularly, many may recognize themselves in this comment. Sometimes when I hear this sort of remark, and if it seems appropriate, I might respond in this way, *You know, there are people that the Church hasn't 'got' but that God has got, and I think there are also people that the Church has got, that God hasn't got!*[11] This seems especially apt at the moment as this chapter is being written at the same time as the Royal Commission into Child Abuse has released some appalling data on the extent of abuse in recent decades. We will need to deal with sin in the Church later.

So this brings us to the heart of the matter, and the real purpose of this field guide: what makes a person a *good Catholic*? Is it just a question of religious observance or is there more involved? In exploring this question, we will first need to grapple with the concept of spirituality.

> *What do you think are the most important attributes of a good person? A good Christian? A good Catholic?*

---

11   I cannot recall the source but I believe that this statement is originally attributed to St Augustine.

What is Spirituality?

Spirituality is a very broad idea as well as a universal human experience—everyone has spirituality, but not everyone *has religion*.

> *'Everyone has a spirituality ...'* do you agree?

Spirituality is something that shapes each one of us. It defines how we connect to others and the world around us. To see how much has been written on spirituality, and the wide variety of possibilities or choices available, just walk into a bookshop or do a Google search on the word. It can all be very confusing! So once again, there can only be a very brief overview in this field guide, focussing on what a genuine Catholic spirituality might entail.

Discovering our individual spirituality typically involves a search for meaning of life shaped by questions such as the following (several of which will already be familiar from the previous chapter, *Some Big Questions*).

Am *I* a good person?

What is the meaning of *my* suffering?

What is *my* connection to the world around me?

Do things happen to *me* or others for a reason?

How can *I* live *my* life in the best way possible?

Spirituality can therefore start, and even stop, with an individual person. Maybe in theory everyone could have a unique, individual spirituality. However, by its very nature, a healthy spirituality will seek connection with others, and this is where religion can potentially be very helpful. At its core, a healthy religion nurtures shared or communal spiritualities with the wonderful advantage of being *free to learn* from others thus not having to *reinvent the wheel* ourselves.

> *You might like to stop here for a few minutes and list how you like to nurture your spirit, or the core of who you are.*

Our spirituality is like a driving force that deeply sustains us and gives our lives enduring meaning. Daily we can nurture our spirituality with a whole range of spiritual practices such as: prayer, quiet reflection, reading inspiring books, music, enjoying nature, and attending church services when available.

Nurturing our spirituality is very important. It's just *so easy* to be consumed by the everyday, the here and now, that we end up starving our souls, our inner lives, and just operate unfeelingly on *auto pilot*. We become *soul-less* people, often just drifting and rudderless. Sometimes when we starve our souls, we also end up being very lonely because we can push others away with cold and robot-like behaviour.

However, when we nurture our souls, we create more joy in our lives which can become almost like a song, flowing easily and in tune. The more fully we engage in what feeds our souls, the happier we feel, and the greater the inner strength we can draw on when the unexpected happens, as it undoubtedly will.

Four Essentials

A well-known and very gifted, modern Catholic writer, Ronald Rolheiser, proposes four non-negotiable essentials or pillars of a genuine Christian spirituality.[12] These are:

1. Private prayer and private morality,
2. Social justice,
3. Mellowness of heart and spirit, and,
4. Community as a key element of true worship.

Let's briefly review these.

Private prayer and private morality: In essence, these will both shape and nourish our individual relationships with God, how we individually stand before God and, particularly, whether this stance has integrity in relation to keeping the Commandments. The Bible makes it very clear, *If you love me, you will keep my commandments* (John 14:15) and it is only in doing so that our prayers will not be an illusion.

---

12   Rolheiser, R. (1998) *Seeking Spirituality: Guidelines for a Christian Spirituality for the Twenty First Century.* London: Hodder & Stoughton. Pp 50-68

Rolheiser writes, ... *we will make progress in the spiritual life only if we, daily, do an extended period of private prayer, and only if we practice a scrupulous vigilance in regard to all the moral areas within our private lives.*[13]

Living in remote areas doesn't always make it any easier to pray regularly. As long ago as the time of the Desert Fathers, it was recognised that *there is no labour greater than that of prayer to God* (Abba Agathon). He recognised that every time we want to pray, there seems to be something (or someone?) trying to prevent or disrupt us. It is therefore very important to persevere in our prayer lives in order to remain centred on God as much as possible and thus give lasting context, meaning and depth to the business—and busyness—of each day.

> *Do you have a regular and private prayer routine? What priority does prayer have in your daily life?*

One spiritual practice, steeped in prayer—used by countless thousands over the centuries to nourish their journey into more loving relationships with God, and with others—is found in Ignatian spirituality. This practice is known as the *Examen,* essentially a prayerful review of the day, undertaken once or twice per day, to reflect on what has been happening and to discern the movement of God's spirit in the circumstances in which we find ourselves. It can be compared to *pressing the rewind button* and playing back the events of the day to learn from them. There are many on-line resources available to guide and assist you with this practice, such as: https://www.ignatianspirituality.com/ignatian-prayer/the-examen.

Social Justice: Caring for those less fortunate than ourselves lies at the very heart of the Gospel that Jesus preached and witnessed to throughout his public ministry; he was often found at the fringes of society with the sick, the poor, the outcasts. All the Gospels are very clear on this and there is no scope for any doubt—we will all be judged

---

13   Rolheiser, R. (1998), 61

on how we treat the poor, because how we treat the poor is how we treat God.

As Rolheiser writes, ... *as Jesus himself makes clear, there can be no real relationship with him when the poor are neglected and injustice abounds. When we make spirituality essentially a privatised thing, cut off from the poor .... and demands for justice ... it soon degenerates into mere private therapy ... or worse still, an unhealthy clique.*[14]

Looking out for one another is something that people in the bush tend to do very well. When a neighbour is in trouble people often rally around to help and assist in any way they can. I have certainly witnessed some incredible outpourings of generosity in cash and in kind when there has been an accident or disaster such as the current long-running drought. The challenge for everyone is to keep this spirit of compassion and care for one another burning brightly all the time, even when we feel as if we have nothing to give because we ourselves are overburdened and stressed.

Isn't it true that when we are in such a place, doing something for someone else, who may well be feeling even worse than we do, often greatly lifts our spirits and we are the ones then being blessed.

> *Can you think of some examples where your own troubles seemed to lessen or even disappear when you chose to help someone else?*

Mellowness of heart and spirit: Perhaps the best way to understand this non- negotiable essential of Christian spirituality is with a question, *Will we convert the world with pushy, driven Christians, with a message they just have to sell, or with Christians who, knowing their own sinfulness, are operating from a place of compassion and gratitude for all the blessings that they have received?*[15] Kindness, compassion, gratitude and warmth are what shape a mellow heart and spirit.

---

14 Rolheiser, R. (1998), 63
15 Rolheiser, R. (1998), 64

Rolheiser, drawing on another famous Christian writer, Julian of Norwich, suggests that God sits in heaven, not *wired*, neurotic, anxious or bitter as we sometimes are but is, instead, *completely relaxed, looking with marvellous sympathy.* [16] I love this image!

Mellowness of heart and spirit may not be a description that many people of the bush would easily relate to. Instead, being tough, resilient and knowing their own minds—and showing this—might be seen as more appropriate, especially for men. However, operating from a disposition where kindness, compassion, gratitude and warmth are in play may well be a source of great and lasting strength, not only for that individual but, perhaps more importantly, for all those around him or her.

Community as a key Element of True Worship: We have already noted the danger of *going it alone* in a previous chapter. Now it is necessary to *up the ante* as it were, by asserting that participation in a Christian community is a non-negotiable essential of Christian spirituality. Without involvement in a Christian community, Rolheiser notes that an individual, no matter how sincere their spiritual seeking, *lives the un-confronted life [often with] more private fantasy than real faith ... [while] real conversion demands ... [involvement]... in both the muck and the grace of actual church life. Spirituality is about a **communal** search for the face of God.* [17] Not an easy position to accept for those who want God but don't want the church.

> '*... participation in a Christian community is a non-negotiable essential of Christian spirituality'.*
> *Do you agree?*

Spirituality without religion is spirit without form ... and religion without spirituality is form without substance. [18]

---

16   Rolheiser, R. (1998), 64

17   Rolheiser, R. (1998), 66

18   Tacey, David (2015) *Spirituality and Religion in a Secular World*, Power Point Presentation, accessible via: https://www.slideshare.net/leonardo.correa/spirituality-and-religion-in-a-secular-world

This photo was taken during an ecumenical Christmas liturgy at Perryvale Station, the most remote cattle station in Etheridge Shire, Far North Queensland

The fact that gathering for communal worship and prayer is so difficult for many people in the bush is the very reason this guide has been produced. While attendance at church services—the relatively rare occasions that they might be available—remains important, there are also other potential options available for intentionally gathering to support one another in matters of faith, recognising that Christian faith has always had a communal dimension. These might include:

- family or community liturgies (some examples are included as Appendices in this guide), especially for important occasions like Christmas, Anzac Day and the like,

- participation in Bible study or prayer groups with like-minded neighbours noting that these can either be face to face or via on-line video/voice technologies such as Skype,

- prayer chains, defined groups of people who are called upon to pray for someone in difficulties or for a particular situation possibly affecting a number of people, and,

- using social media (such as a special Facebook group) to share about matters of faith and create a sense of community.

Each of these communal activities requires at least one person who is prepared to organise the activity and gather family, neighbours or friends together. Understandably, many (if not most) people are hesitant to undertake such a lead or coordinating role because they do not want to thrust themselves forward thinking that they might come across as a *holy Joe or Jill*, better than others, or, because they are afraid they might not lead the activity properly. However, if any leader or coordinator role is thought of as providing a ***service for the benefit of others***, a service which is offered humbly and with prayerful preparation beforehand, then we can be sure that God will be present through grace to support us. Perfection is not required.

> *Have you ever thought of gathering your family, friends or neighbours together into a communal activity such as one of these? If not, why? Do you think you might like to try doing so in future? If so, help is available.*

The Importance of the Mass

Following on naturally from the preceding paragraphs on the communal aspects of a genuine spirituality, it is appropriate to consider the importance of the Mass in this regard. The Second Vatican Council (held in the early 1960s) affirmed the Mass—or Eucharist as it is also referred to—as the *summit and fountain* of the whole of the Church's life and activity. In saying this, the Council expressed the faith of the Church that there is no higher form of worship which could be offered to God.

The Mass has very ancient roots, namely the Last Supper which Jesus celebrated with his disciples on the eve of His passion and death. From the apostles themselves and from within the first Christian communities in the first decades after Jesus' death and resurrection, the ritual blessing, breaking and sharing of bread, and the blessing and sharing of the cup, have formed an unbroken and consistent tradition within the Catholic Church for nearly 2000 years down to what we now recognise and celebrate as the Mass in the present day.

> *What priority do you place on participating in the Mass when it is available in your community or area?*
>
> *How do you think this might change in future?*

There are many, many pages that could be written about the Mass, much more than is possible or appropriate for a short guide such as this. However, it is possible to propose some of the key elements that make the Mass so special:

- It was instituted by Jesus himself, who also said very clearly, ***Do this in remembrance of me*** (Luke 22:19).
- The Mass allows us to encounter Christ Jesus in both the words of Scripture, and as a real presence in Communion; something we are asked to accept in faith as the appearance of the communion bread and wine do not change.
- In coming to Mass, we *come as we are*, and offer ourselves to God just as we are—with all our strengths and weaknesses—together with the community's gifts of bread and wine which are brought to the altar during the Offertory procession.
- Just as we pray together with the priest to consecrate these gifts to become the Body and Blood of Christ for us, we also humbly ask that we ourselves be blessed and consecrated anew as His disciples.
- The Mass then culminates with Holy Communion where we are nourished—body and soul—by Christ Himself, so that we may become more Christ-like.
- When Mass is concluded, we are then sent out to bring the Christ we have received into the situations in which we each find ourselves: family, work, and so on. Sometimes this is referred to as being Eucharist for others.

- Mass is a community event, drawing people together as members of the Church into an assembly with only one purpose—to follow Christ and to witness to His ongoing presence in the world. In this unique way, the Church becomes a visible sign—or Sacrament—of Christ's ongoing mission for the salvation of all humankind.

For a detailed description of all the elements and stages of the Mass, please refer to the following link: http://www.usccb.org/about/public-affairs/backgrounders/structure-and-meaning-of-the-mass-backgrounder.cfm.

Practising the Presence of God

Now that we have considered important aspects of a *Christian spirituality*, with some emphasis on the communal or shared spiritual life, it is appropriate to once again highlight what is essential for all Christians—developing *a personal relationship* with the Living God as revealed in, and through, Jesus the Christ. In faith we believe that God is always present to us but perhaps we are not often present to God, and so the relationship suffers.

For many years now, I have had in the front of my rather worn Bible—worn from age and not so much from the number of times I have read it through—a number of tips about making God's presence more real in our everyday lives, with their many often unexpected twists and turns, and ups and downs. I don't remember which book/s I read to produce this list but nevertheless wish to share it with you in case it is of some interest – perhaps better titled as *practising being present to God*:

- have a *daily quiet time* for prayer and, perhaps more importantly, to just sit still and be,
- remember to invite God into the ordinary, every-day things we do (think of it like a *partnership* ... talk to God like we chat with a mate or co-worker),

Bringing the presence of God into clearer focus....

- ***cultivate a praising heart*** (remember to say thank you, and to praise God for the many gifts we have received, and take the time to count them),

- ***watch for the unusual/unexpected*** (God often tries to get our attention this way, and we can so easily miss these if we are not attentive—luckily it doesn't all depend on us as God can always find another way),

- ***read the Bible regularly*** (yes, it was written a long time ago, but it is has ancient wisdom which is inspired by God and thus ageless, always capable of stimulating, guiding and even challenging us in ways that could be life changing, or perhaps just enable us to work through what is happening in our lives (please refer also to the next chapter which discusses the Bible)),

- ***share God's gifts*** (covered under the social justice discussion above),

- ***fellowship or connecting with others*** (covered above under the community or communal aspects of a genuine Christian spirituality),

- *look after oneself* (we can be so focussed on our responsibilities towards others, or work, and so on, that we forget to look after ourselves by having some *down time*; if we are rarely able to be still and revitalise, we will steadily deplete ourselves physically, emotionally and spiritually and eventually we will burn-out or break down altogether), and,
- *break decisively with all known sin:*
  - ~ Have I been truthful and honest?
  - ~ Have I allowed bitterness to take root?
  - ~ Have I been impure?
  - ~ Have I sought God's glory or my own?
  - ~ Has love been my motive in everything?

There is another practice, but I am reluctant to share it because I don't think I have really ever tried to put it into practice myself. It is this: *joyfully and willingly open doors to trials and tribulations.* Really? Perhaps that is only for those on the path to sainthood!

Some Catholic Spiritualities

Within the Catholic tradition, we are truly blessed to have available to us a very, very wide range of spiritualities each with their associated charisms (or styles) which have been practiced through many centuries and passed down to us. There really seems to be something for everybody. Sadly, however, much Catholic practice and formation has become somewhat *one dimensional*, not really opening up for most people some of these very rich (and proven) spiritualities with their specific insights and practices. Here is just a small sample:

- The *Desert Fathers and Mothers* chose to live in the wilderness and deserts of Egypt and other places some 1600-1700 years ago, away from the hustle and bustle of both state and church. Their very challenging spirituality led them to live their lives stripped to the bare essentials to make room for God. Many of their sayings and insights survive to this day.

Veronique

This illustration depicts some structure, also suggesting stained glass, associated with established Catholic spiritualties overlaid on an Australian bush setting

- **Benedictine Spirituality** is based on the teachings and the rule of St. Benedict of Nursia (480-543 AD) who established the first monastic order, the Benedictines, which also survives into the present day across the world. The basic premise of the Benedictine 'Rule' is all that is needed, is to be faithful to finding God in the ordinary circumstances of daily life, whether one lives in a monastery or at home with a busy and noisy family.

- **Franciscan Spirituality** is based on the teachings and example of Sr Francis of Assisi (1181-1226 AD) who established the Franciscans, an order which also survives to this day. Franciscan spirituality emphasised the goodness of God and the goodness of creation which is the outpouring of God's love into the universe. Franciscans call creation, the *mirror of God*.

- **Carmelite Spirituality** has been practiced since the 12th century by both men and women, ordained and non-ordained. This is a desert spirituality drawing on the experiences of the Old

Testament prophet Elijah, who fled into the desert to escape persecution for being God's true prophet and doing things which did not endear him to the secular rulers. In the desert, Elijah went into a deep depression, because his self-esteem was shattered and he could see no way out. However, it was here in the desert that he encountered God and recovered. The best advice ever given in the Scriptures for someone suffering from misplaced anger, depression and feelings of hopelessness is what was said to Elijah by God in 1 Kings 19:11, i.e., *Go out, get up and stand on the mountain top before your God.*

- *Ignatian Spirituality* grew from the teachings of St. Ignatius of Loyola, who lived from 1491-1556 AD and founded the Society of Jesus, known more commonly as Jesuits. His work, Spiritual Exercises, a collection of his prayers and insights, is considered one of the most influential books on the spiritual life ever written and continues to be followed and practiced into the present day by people throughout the world, nourishing their souls in the *everyday* and the mundane. Ignatian spirituality recognises that God is always, and in all things, present to each and every one of us: in our relationships, in our work, in nature. We don't have to do anything special or withdraw into a monastery to find God!

- *The Spirituality of St. Mary of the Cross Mackillop* is based on the life and witness of Mary Mackillop, Australia's first saint who lived from 1842 till 1909. She established the Sisters of St. Joseph which continues into the present day inspired by her spirituality and example. *Today Josephite spirituality can be seen as an energy that seeks right relationships with God, others, self and the earth. Wherever we are, in town or country, city or mountains or far from home in other lands, we trust that we will find God's meaning, purpose and vitality daily in whatever we do.*[19]

---

19   Extracted from the Sisters of St. Joseph website.

- *The Society of St. Vincent de Paul* was founded in France by a 20 year old university student named Frederic Ozanam in 1833. It was established by like-minded young people who wished to put their faith into action by serving the less fortunate; the poor and needy. Now a worldwide Catholic lay organisation, it is still fuelled by the same compassionate outlook, enthusiasm and vision. Across Australia, there are thousands of people who share their time, compassion and energy to make a difference, through the many works of the Society, in the lives of disadvantaged people.

- *Indigenous Spirituality* in Australia has very ancient origins, many thousands of years before the emergence of the Catholic spiritualities briefly described above. In the words of St. Pope John Paul II—addressing the indigenous people of Australia at Alice Springs in November 1986—not only was the Spirit of God with them throughout this time, but the stories of the Dreamtime legends, *speak powerfully of the great mysteries of human life, its frailty, its need for help, its closeness to spiritual powers and the value of the human person.*[20] Importantly, he then went on to say, *The Church herself in Australia will not be fully the Church that Jesus wants her to be until you have made your contribution to her life and until that contribution has been joyfully received by others.* Integrating key elements of indigenous spirituality—such as the importance of silence and connection to the land—into the life of our Church, and into the various streams of Catholic spirituality more broadly, remains an important work-in-progress.

> *Are you aware of any other Catholic spiritualities?*
>
> *Which (if any) appeal to you?*

---

20   http://w2.vatican.va/content/john-paul-ii/en/speeches/1986/november/documents/hf_jp-ii_spe_19861129_aborigeni-alice-springs-australia.html

An evocative painting of the Nativity by an unknown Aboriginal artist. This painting was purchased by the author at Daly River in the Northern Territory in 1991.

Summary

In this chapter we have explored some key aspects of spirituality, and provided some examples of Catholic spiritualities which are differentiated from one another and also from the mainstream, or parish life, of the Church. When—as is the case in the Gulf Savannah Parish, and probably in many other rural and remote parishes—this mainstream life is not often accessible or available, this doesn't of course mean that *nothing* is available. Without detracting from the centrality of the Mass, what this chapter has sought to demonstrate is that there is a very rich and very broad range of Catholic spiritualities (and associated practices) which can inform, nurture and sustain our individual and communal journeys towards God everyday single day of our lives, but only if we choose to engage with them when we are 'out in the paddocks'.

This chapter also offers, for consideration and prayerful reflection, four foundational and non-negotiable pillars for our Christian and thus Catholic lives: our private prayer and private morality, engaging in social justice, maintaining mellowness of heart and spirit, and, participation in community as a key element of true worship.

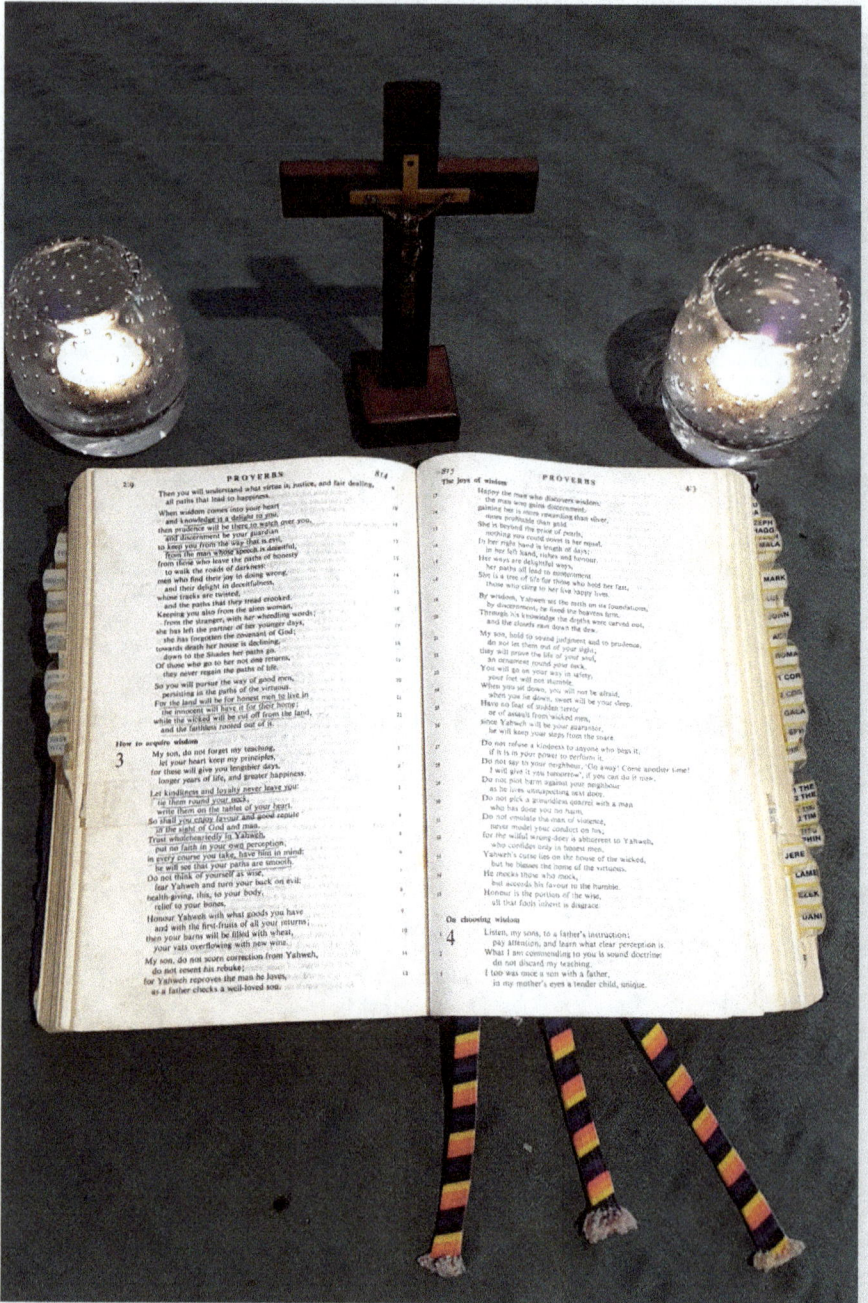

My well-worn and marked Jerusalem Bible which has been my companion since 1985.

THE BIBLE AS THE WORD OF GOD

Introduction

In brief, the purpose of this chapter is to introduce readers to the Bible which remains the most widely read book in the world; a Number One best seller position it has held for a very

> *Before proceeding, you might like to make some notes on what you understand the Bible to be?*

long time. At the same time, whilst one might think that the Bible itself would be a pre-eminent source of unity amongst Christians, it actually has been a major focus of division over the centuries. This is in large part due to different understandings of what the Bible is and what the Bible is not, as this chapter will try to make clear.

What is the Bible?

A Story of God's Revelation and Invitation to enter into a Relationship

In its very essence, the Bible is the story of God's revelation, initially to a particular society of people—namely the Jews or Israelites—and then in and through Jesus the Christ, to all people everywhere, and in all times, irrespective of race or culture. It is important to recognise that, whilst Christians believe that this story of revelation fully discloses the *nature* of God, especially as a God of infinite and unconditional love, it can *never be the whole or complete* story of God's revelation to **all** of humanity. God, being God, is infinitely free to reveal Godself in infinite ways, with a special way for every unique person in the particular circumstances in which he or she finds themselves.

Therein lies the entire purpose of God's self-revelation—to invite *every person* into a life-giving relationship with God, a relationship with mutual obligations which are founded on love and respect, thankfully not so much **our** love and respect, but **God's**. The Bible is a collection of stories about how these relationships unfold, relationships between God and individuals, families, communities or whole societies, where the relationships work well, and where they completely break down with the resultant consequences. Yes, they are ancient stories—the last book of the Bible, *Revelations*, was written by about the end of the first century, some 1900 years ago—but if we read the Bible prayerfully and mindfully, its texts can be ever new and always remain relevant.

Here is but one small example, attributed to words spoken by Jesus (Gospel of Matthew 6: 25-33):

> Therefore I tell you, do not worry about your life, what you will eat or what you will drink, or about your body, what you will wear. Is not life more than food and the body more than clothing? Look at the birds of the air; they neither sow nor reap nor gather into barns, and yet your heavenly Father feeds them. Are you not of more value than they? And can any of you by worrying add a single hour to your span of life? And why do you worry about clothing? Consider the lilies of the field, how they grow; they neither toil nor spin, yet I tell you, even Solomon in all his glory was not clothed like one of these. But if God so clothes the grass of the field, which is alive today and tomorrow is thrown into the oven, will he not much more clothe you—you of little faith? Therefore do not worry, saying, 'What will we eat?' or 'What will we drink?' or 'What will we wear?' For it is the pagans who strive for all these things; and indeed your heavenly Father knows that you need all these things. But strive first for the kingdom of

God and his righteousness, and all these things will be given to you as well.

Perhaps this is a message that our money focussed, consumerist society may very well need to reflect on from time to time, perhaps also asking the question, *Why do we do what we do?* This text is but one small example of how the timeless wisdom of God's self-revelation in the Bible transcends any context of time, space or culture and can speak very clearly into our current situations.

> *What is your favourite Bible passage? Why do you think you especially connect with it?*

Often during Bible studies in small groups, the same short Bible text can be interpreted and applied in as many different ways as the number of people in the room. Similarly, when I was in a group of aspirants preparing to be ordained as Permanent Deacons, we regularly delivered practice homilies to one another ... before being let loose on any unsuspecting flocks! Although based on the same Bible texts, our homilies were *always* radically different. These examples of different interpretations of exactly the same texts confirm that the Bible offers inexhaustible spiritual and religious riches which will be ever new depending on where and when it is being read, by whom and what their particular circumstances are.

Regular Bible readers are sometimes heard to exclaim (in jest!), When did they put that sentence in there? It wasn't there last time I read this section! Of course, it was there, but God reveals specific ideas and truths when He knows we need to hear them.

Human Story, Divine Inspiration

Christians have different beliefs and opinions about who actually wrote the Bible. Some believe that the Bible consists of God's very own words and therefore cannot have any errors whatsoever, even against the findings of science. (Please also refer to the section discussing faith and/or reason, above.) For these Christians, any verse in the Bible can be used in isolation to communicate what God has to say on any particular issue. However, this approach causes enormous difficulties for many people, not the least of these being that, taken in isolation, very many contradictory themes can be found in different Bible texts.

In this context, what many people may not be aware of is that the Bible is not a book in the common understanding of this word, namely that it is written by one author in a particular place and time, like most of the stories in both fiction and non-fiction books in circulation today. In contrast the Bible is a collection of books (the word Bible comes from the Greek word *biblia* meaning books) which were written over approximately 1000 years, in different places and all by unknown authors in widely different circumstances or what are technically referred to as *historical contexts*.

How does the knowledge that the Bible was written over such a long period by mostly unknown authors impact your understanding of the Bible?

Major Christian churches believe that the entire Bible is divinely inspired to provide an integrated account of God's self-revelation and how the resulting divine-human relationship evolved in particular historical and cultural settings over more than 1,000 years. Nevertheless, the written accounts in the Bible are always constrained by the limitations of the authors, human beings just like us. No human being, no matter how learned or wise, is capable of adequately expressing the mystery of God's nature, actions or will.

Hebrew and Christian Scriptures

As noted above, books of the Bible contain foundational texts for two of the world's major religions: Judaism and Christianity. The Bible is also held with great respect by followers of Islam, as providing a background historical and prophetic context for what is believed to be God's revelation through the prophet Mohammed.

Historically, the Bible has been divided into two main sections: the Old Testament, by far the larger part of the Bible, which is concerned with God's revelation to, and relationship with, the Jews (or Hebrews), up until the time Jesus was born, and, the New Testament which is all about God's self-revelation in and through His Son, Jesus the Christ, and the emergence of early Christian communities in the first century. More recently, and acknowledging that for Jewish people their revered books of scripture[21] are certainly not *Old*, a more respectful approach has emerged and this refers to the Bible as consisting of the Hebrew and Christian Scriptures, rather than the *Old* and *New* Testaments.

Importantly, for all Christians, the Bible—and thus the story of God's self-revelation—consists of *both* the Hebrew and Christian Scriptures. Interestingly, it took several hundred years for the books in the Bible, as we know it today, to be agreed within the Church and even now, Protestant Bibles only contain 39 books in the Hebrew Scriptures while Catholic Bibles have 46, including the books known as the Apocrypha, the authenticity of which is disputed by both Hebrew and Protestant scholars and theologians.

What the Bible is Not!

Clearly from the discussion above, the Bible is not a history book, and it was not written down immediately, on the spot, by people walking around with notebooks like newspaper reporters do today to feed the 24 hour news cycle. While the Bible certainly contains historical accounts—which have been at least partially verified by other sources and by archaeology—it also includes a variety of writings: myths, homilies, poetry, statements of faith and beliefs, prayers, parables, laws, songs and wise sayings, to name just a few. These all need to be distinguished otherwise what was written down as a mythical narrative by an ancient author might be—very wrongly—interpreted today as a historical fact. Once again, this is where a fundamental or literal

---

21   *Scripture* comes from the Latin word *scripturae*, meaning writings

understanding of the Bible as the inerrant Word of God, dictated word for word by Godself, can cause so much difficulty, and even present Christianity as somewhat crazy—disconnected from reality, from reason itself, and from the real concerns of ordinary people trying to find enduring meaning for their lives.

Are there different versions of the Bible?

Yes there are many different versions of the Bible. Quite apart from the fact that the Bible has been completely translated into over 400 languages (a work that is ongoing) just within the English language there are well over 50 different translations. The reasons why there are so many include:

- The changing nature of the English language: to see a clear example of this, consider the opening sentence of the passage from Matthew quoted at the beginning of this chapter, in the King James Version of the Bible written some 400 years ago, *Therefore I say unto you, Take no thought for your life, what ye shall eat, or what ye shall drink; nor yet for your body, what ye shall put on. Is not the life more than meat, and the body than raiment?*,

- Changes in culture, such as efforts in recent times to use inclusive language, not all of which have been well received, and,

- The particular circumstances and spiritual/theological preferences of the translators. An example is that some Protestant versions reject the proposition that the Bible is anything other than the inerrant word of God. They therefore seek to minimise in their translations any differences between the books or texts of the Bible, and also tend to dismiss the results of modern, scholarly studies of scripture.

So, which versions should Catholics use? Personally, I have two hard copies of the Bible that I use regularly. The first of these is a very well-worn Jerusalem Bible which I have had for over 30 years and has been marked-up. This Bible feels like a very comfortable old pair of shoes—it is familiar and easy to 'put on' or use. The other version is an ecumenical study Bible which I have found to be very useful for really appreciating the historical context of each Book, and indeed the entire Bible. It is filled with very useful notes and maps etc. to really help with understanding when each book was written, by whom, why and in what particular historical setting. This is the New Revised Standard Version (NRSV) which has been accepted by most Christian denominations. It is titled *The New Oxford Annotated Bible, NRSV, with the Apocrypha* and the full reference is below.[22]

Both the Jerusalem Bible and the NRSV translations have been formally approved for use by Catholics, and there are other approved versions as well. However, if you have another version at home, why not use it, especially if it is a family heirloom. Just be aware in doing so that there may be some biases in the translation for the reasons noted above.

The Importance of the Bible

Pope Paul VI in 1965, in his encyclical *Dei Verbum (Word of God)* presented the teaching of the Church on the importance of the Bible not only in the life of the Church but also for every individual. He wrote:

> The sacred synod also earnestly and especially urges all the Christian faithful, especially Religious, to learn by frequent reading of the divine Scriptures the "excellent knowledge of Jesus Christ" (Phil. 3:8). For ignorance of the Scriptures is ignorance of Christ. Therefore, they should gladly put themselves in touch with the sacred text itself, whether it be through the liturgy, rich in the divine word, or through devotional reading, or through instructions suitable for the purpose ... And let them remember that prayer should accompany the reading of Sacred Scripture, so that God and man may talk together; for we speak to Him when we pray; we hear Him when we read the divine saying. (*Dei Verbum* 25)

---

22 Coogan, M. D. (2010). *The New Oxford Annotated Bible*, New Revised Standard Version with the Apochrypha. Oxford, USA: Oxford University Press

How do I read the Bible?

Straight Through

If you have never done so, you could just read the Bible straight through so that you can become familiar, in general terms, with the story of God's revelation through the Hebrews and then in, and through, Jesus the Christ. You might however, like to start with the Christian Scriptures (New Testament) and then read the Hebrew Scriptures (Old Testament), remembering that, for a Christian, both are important in what they reveal about God, and humanity.

There are also a variety of *reading plans* available to allow you to read the Bible in a more structured way over one year. (Please refer to the resources section below).

A More Formal Study

Perhaps there is a particular book of the Bible, or an extract or text that you become very interested in understanding, and connecting with, more fully through a more formal study. Thankfully there are a number of valuable resources available to assist. These include:

- Study Bibles, such as the Oxford Study Bible already mentioned,
- scholarly commentaries on particular books of the Bible,
- Bible dictionaries which explain ancient terms and provide detailed information on places, cultures societies, and the like (all to assist with gaining a better understanding), and,
- workbooks for personal or group use.

If you are at all unsure about which resources might be appropriate, just ask your Priest, Deacon or Religious.

Prayerful Immersion in a Particular Text

This way of reading the Bible allows a particular Scripture text to read us in the way it connects with our own particular situations, and events in our lives, as they are on that day. We open ourselves to the presence of God speaking through the Scriptures into our own concerns and memories,

Have you ever realised that the same Spirit present and who inspired the ancient author of a Bible text is also present when you read it from the perspective of your own life and situation?

Is there any limit to the ways in which a Bible text can be read, understood and/or applied?

our relationships and our hopes for the future. This is a slow, contemplative approach steeped in prayer so that the text truly becomes for each of us the *living Word of God*, uniquely spoken into our souls and thus into our lives.

Immersion is the goal here, not scheduling!

Clearly, this is the most important way of reading the Bible; to take the time to really *chew over* and pray into a chosen piece of scripture text so that we might be able to hear with our souls what God might be trying to tell us. One way to do this is through what is known as *Lectio Divina* (Divine Reading).

Lectio Divina

This way of prayerfully reading a Scripture text is as follows:

Choose a text you wish to pray. This might be from the daily readings for the Mass or from a particular book of the Bible you are working through. The choice is really yours. Perhaps it is the text that you have somehow been led to by God! Try to avoid any expectations or goals as to the amount of text you must cover.

Get comfortable and become silent. This can perhaps be achieved by just taking some slow deep breaths, or whatever works for you to enjoy silence for a while.

Read your chosen text slowly and gently. Stop at any phrase or word that seems to be really connecting with you, and quietly suggesting that it is what you need just now.

Stay with this word or phrase, ponder it, *chew it over*. Allow it to work its way deep within to your inner self and whatever it is that you are most aware of; it could be a memory, an experience (good or bad) earlier that day, a relationship, a hope or a concern for someone, or for the future, and so on. You might then invite God to enter into this *rumination* or pondering; keep still and be open to what God might be saying.

Speak to God as the One who loves you unconditionally. Thank God for the insights you have discovered during this meditation on the Word of scripture, and ask that, with God's grace, that they might bless and transform you more fully into a fuller life lived God's Way.

Rest quietly in God's love. Have faith in God's closeness to you, eventually letting God's Spirit gently guide you; perhaps you might be led to return to the text, or to continue resting in God's presence, or to conclude *Lectio* for now. Try not to 'push things along' as God remains close to us whether we are active or receptive spiritually. Rejoice in the knowledge that God is with you in both words and silence, in spiritual activity and inner receptivity.

The ***only goal*** of *Lectio Divina* is to place us in the presence of God by prayerfully immersing ourselves in Scripture texts. *Lectio Divina* should never be approached anxiously, thinking that we are not doing it correctly; it is not a test or a performance which can, in any way, be assessed. Perhaps the best way to approach *Lectio Divina*, therefore, is just to enter into it, to practise it and LET GO to LET GOD.

Bible Study Groups

While probably not within the common, lived experience of most Catholics (or Christians) in our more isolated rural and remote areas, small groups—coming together to study a book or text of the Bible—have been quite commonplace in larger Christian communities or parishes for many years. Sometimes such groups come together for a set time only (for example, during Lent) and then disband. In the Gulf Savannah Parish, Lenten bible study groups have been very successfully conducted via Skype, grouping people separated over vast distances.

If you have never participated in a small Bible study group, why not give it a try when the next opportunity arises? From personal experience, participation in such groups has invariably been life-giving and deeply enriching through the sharing of personal insights, understandings and experiences. Some people say that faith is a *private thing* and, therefore, are very reluctant to talk about their faith and the way they practice it. Sure, when new Bible study groups start up, it's a little awkward and uncomfortable as people get to know one another. Experience, however, has shown time and time again that this doesn't last very long and hearts, minds, and mouths all start to open as barriers fall down in a trusting and supportive environment, especially when people start to realise that they are not alone in trying to find meaning and a deeper faith.

Yes, some people say faith is a private thing. Others say an isolated Christian is a paralysed Christian, as noted above.

Some Useful Resources.

Bible Reading Plans for 2018:

https://www.ligonier.org/blog/bible-reading-plans/

Complete On-Line Bibles (over 150 Translations):

https://www.biblegateway.com/

Commentaries:

There are far too many commentaries to list, and some will be more suitable than others; it is strongly suggested that you discuss which may be most suitable with your Clergy or Religious.

This photo is of Cobbold Gorge, located near Forsayth in the Gulf Savannah. There was not a single ripple on the water and not a sound to be heard.

SILENCE—A SPECIAL GIFT OF THE BUSH ... AND THE ESSENCE OF SPIRITUALITY

Be still and know that I am God! (Psalm 46:10)

Introduction

How often do you give yourself the gift of silence?

If you can't get to the bush, how can you bring the silence of the outback into your life?

Did you know that the invitation to stop for a while, to be still and silent—to create a quiet space in which we can just take a big breath and get in touch with ourselves at a deeper level—is present in all the major world religions? More than that, and as this brief overview will show, silence is also a spiritual practice of one of the oldest cultures in the world and present in our midst, that of our Indigenous Australians. Silence and stillness are also entered into as a form of wordless prayer which can be both restorative and empowering, especially when we are unable to find the right words to pray for whatever reason, particularly when we feel exhausted with the daily demands on our time and our energy.

These are some of the matters that this chapter will seek to address.

A Personal Note...

Sometimes, when I am driving on some long, deserted road or track in the Gulf Savannah Parish, I feel moved to stop the car, switch off the engine, get out and just listen to ... NOTHING ... except, perhaps, from time to time, the intermittent call of a solitary bird. God sometimes seems very close when I stop and immerse myself in such marvellous silence.

I also remember intentionally doing something similar years ago when driving through a vast, spinifex covered plain in Western Australia. I stopped the car somewhere deep in that wilderness with my car being the only artificial object visible from horizon to horizon. The silence was heavy and with it came a sense, not only of the timelessness of this vast land we call Australia, but also of God's timeless presence in creation which goes on quietly every day.

The spiritual value of being silent or being still is something that I have come to understand and appreciate a lot more as I have grown older, helped along by some wonderful insights of both ancient spiritual masters and modern practitioners. However, I am still on training wheels! Recently my Spiritual Director gave me an extract from a book by Laurence Freeman, titled *Meditation and Christian Prayer*, in which he compares our spiritual lives to old-fashioned wagon-wheels, with the spokes representing different styles of prayer and faith practice. Very perceptively he writes:

> At the hub of the wheel, at the centre of prayer, you find stillness. Without the stillness of the hub, the wheel cannot turn. Without stillness at the centre, there could be no movement or growth at the circumference. The quality of our activity—of our busy active lives—depends on the stillness we find at the centre.

I think that rather than stopping my car, I need to stop my busy life more often, to be silent, to be still, and to let my soul rest for a while. Perhaps it is like that for you too?

Silent Awareness

This wonderful sunset greeted us one evening in Ravenshoe as we came out of the church after Holy Hour.

Anyone living and working on the cattle stations in the huge Gulf Savannah Parish (and indeed, anywhere on the land somewhere in our large, sparsely populated continent) would probably have experienced moments of *silent awareness*, perhaps a sense of deep peace or a connection with something deeper or bigger than what happens to be going on at the time: a felt connection with nature, the beauty and awe of a glorious sunset, the satisfaction of a great day in the saddle, a night sky filled with stars from horizon to horizon, and so on. These things are always hard to put into words but are definite moments (often gone as quickly as they well-up) of grace or blessing. Some call them *God Moments*.

Be still and know that I am God, says the Psalmist in Psalm 46. How often are we still, quiet, even if just as relaxation and recreation for ourselves? It seems these days that there are almost an infinite number of distractions that keep us from *ever* being silent or still. As well as our televisions, we now have all sorts of social media: Twitter, Facebook and the like which demand our attention, drowning us—if we let them—with trivia. We have smart phones and iPads that enable our bosses, work colleagues, family and friends to email or message us 24x7. As a nation, we are all working longer hours. Noise, busyness, worries, pressures, commuting etc. completely fill our days until we drag ourselves into bed every night only to start it all up again the next morning. We barely have any time to nourish our relationships with those dear to us, let alone to *waste* any time with God.

When it comes to our prayer life, we can be just as driven, trying to somehow squeeze it in somewhere, but struggling to be really present instead of being distracted by what we still have to do that day, or dealing with the aftermath of what has already happened.

I know about these things, because I have been there; many days, I am still there!

Rest in God alone my soul. (Psalm 62:5)

Thankfully, to help us when we are stressed and tired, and when the last thing we want to do is pray a lot of words, there is a form of prayer which is essentially *wordless*. With practice, it helps us to find rest for our weary souls, quietly in the presence of God. This form of prayer has parallels in other religious traditions including Islam, Buddhism and indeed in our own indigenous people. Miriam-Rose Ungunmerr-Baumann, an artist and leader of her people in the remote Aboriginal community of Daly River in the Northern Territory, writes about this:

> *Can you remember any time when you intentionally spent a significant period in silent reflection and awareness, listening for God's voice? How was this experience?*

> What I want to talk about is another special quality of my people.... in our language this quality is called dadirri. It is inner, deep listening and quiet, still awareness. Dadirri recognises the deep spring that is inside us. We call on it and it calls to us. This is the gift that Australia is thirsting for. It is something like

what you call "contemplation". When I experience dadirri, I am made whole again. I can sit on the riverbank or walk through the trees; even if someone close to me has passed away, I can find my peace in this silent awareness...there are deep springs within each of us. Within this deep spring, which is the very Spirit of God, is a sound. The sound of Deep calling to Deep. The sound is the word of God—Jesus.[23]

'Within this deep spring, which is the very Spirit of God, is a sound. The sound of Deep calling to Deep.' (Miriam-Rose Un gunmerr-Baumann)

---

23 Ungunmer-Baumann, Miriam (1988). *Dadirri–Awareness we all should share.* First published in the *Catholic Leader*, February 7th 1989.

Being present to and resting in, God, in stillness and deep silence is a proven practice of *contemplative prayer* with ancient roots, dating back to the earliest centuries of Christianity, but continuing to be practised into the present day as suggested by Miriam Rose. This form of personal prayer has largely evolved as a parallel stream to the liturgical and sacramental life of the Church, but a stream that rarely, if ever, seems to have been promoted from the pulpit. This is a great pity given its proven potential to draw people more deeply into life-giving and life-changing relationships with the Living God.

Please note that the words **meditation** and **contemplation** can sometimes be confused and used interchangeably. Indeed, they can overlap, and one can include the other. Christian meditation, however, mostly involves a more active use of our minds to seek understanding as to the *how* and the *why* of the Christian life. *Contemplation*, on the other hand, is essentially passive, allowing ourselves to be acted upon as we quieten ourselves and open our hearts and minds to the presence of God.

Sometimes, when we are very tired or stressed, ordinary formal or wordy prayer can be very difficult. However, and as stated in the Catholic Catechism:

> contemplative prayer, emphasizing rest and silence, is always available to us. Yet [the fullness of] contemplation [where we find ourselves resting in the gaze of God] is always a gift, a grace. It's not something we achieve, it's something we receive.

Contemplation might be without **effort** on our part, but it is definitely not without **purpose**. By stilling the noise and distractions of our life, and sitting in total surrender, we are inviting God to do the deepest interior work that is most needed.

Interestingly, children and young people can really connect with this form of prayer and indeed some Diocese (e.g. Townsville) incorporate it in the daily prayer life of many Catholic classrooms.

How do I do it?

Here is a very simple guide to Christian contemplative prayer which is directed towards being still in the presence of God, letting our souls rest in God, and opening/emptying our hearts and minds for God to enter. In other words, this prayer is entirely God-oriented. It is opening ourselves up to a deeper, richer encounter so that we might more fully become the people God created each of us to be.

- Try and find a quiet time and place (please note that, rather than driving out of the city or into the outback, it could be as simple as putting your phone on *do not disturb* and shutting the door to your room or office).
- Sit down but always keep your back upright (a straight backed chair is ideal).
- Sit still, relaxed but alert.
- Close your eyes lightly.
- Start by focussing on your breathing; breathe slowly and deeply in, hold it for a moment, and then exhale out slowly.
- Silently, inside your mind, begin to say the sacred word *MA-RA-NA THA* (meaning Come quickly Lord) or choose another word; focus on this word as you repeat it gently and continuously, in time with your breathing.
- Try not to think or imagine anything spiritually—just let yourself rest in your breathing rhythm with the Sacred word.
- If thoughts and images, or outside noises come, don't worry or stress about them; just let them come and go. Gently ignore them and return to the sacred word.
- Try and practice this form of prayer at least once per day; be patient, good things always take time.

After continued practice, you may find that you are starting to receive some of the fruits of contemplation, such as peace, calm, habitual behaviours and addictions having mysteriously declined or disappeared altogether). However, please don't seek or yearn after these as goals in themselves. Just keep faithfully and quietly practising to be still in God's presence, leaving any results or fruits in God's hands.

Some Helpful Resources

http://www.cominghome.org.au/ Christian Meditation for Children and Young People

http://www.christianmeditationaustralia.org/ A Christian meditation resource site

Book by Keating, T. (1992). *Open Mind, Open Heart: The Contemplative Dimension of the Gospel.* Shaftsbury: Element.

An intuitive painting, suggesting that the darkness that is sin is being etched away by the light of God's infinite love and forgiveness.

SIN AND FORGIVENESS

Introduction

On seeing that this chapter deals with sin, is your first reaction to skip it, perhaps thinking that this isn't relevant to me and my circumstances? Or does sin seem like an archaic idea to you, a relic from the past which just used to make many people feel very guilty most of the time, because they could never 'measure up'? Or perhaps some of us are only too well aware of our own disposition to hurt ourselves and to hurt other people, and don't really want to look at our underlying predisposition to weakness, failures ... to sin?

Well, as a counterpoint, it would not be unreasonable to assert that all Christians, since the time of Jesus, have struggled with sin, their own and that of others. Furthermore, and this is very, very important, to be a Christian is also to understand and, hopefully, to have personally experienced the deeply healing power of forgiveness; the forgiveness received from God and from each other. Scripture is very clear: if we are asking for God's forgiveness, we must also extend forgiveness to those who have wronged us.

So, because it is so important a part of being a Christian, the aim of this chapter is to promote at least a basic understanding of sin and its healing remedy, forgiveness.

Sin – A real and present danger...

A genuine Catholic spirituality, incorporating the elements discussed earlier, doesn't develop in splendid isolation, or in some sort of protective bubble, but will be continually challenged by the pervading presence and influence of sin in the world.

Some might be smiling as they read this, perhaps remembering times past when sin seemed to dominate much of both Catholic teaching and understanding on all matters concerning faith. While parish missions by the Redemptorists—and others—often with their 'fire and brimstone' approach to repentance, seem to have long gone, the remnants of these times still shape aspects of Catholic belief and practice in many older Catholics, suggesting—quite wrongly—that God's love is something that we have to *earn* (I have already touched on this in an earlier chapter).

These days, however, there doesn't seem to be as much talk about sin anymore in the liturgical life of our Church, with more emphasis being placed on God's love, compassion and forgiveness. Some argue that, with this focus, the gravity of sin is papered over or trivialised. Where this occurs, it can create an image of God which is unbalanced; God is not just about love and mercy but also about righteousness and justice. Just as in our human lives, adults and even teenagers have to take accountability for our actions, so it is with our spiritual lives, directed towards God. There are consequences for our attitudes and actions (or lack thereof); we only have to look at Biblical passages such as:

- the separation of the sheep from the goats based on the care we have (or have not) provided for those less fortunate than ourselves (Matthew 25: 31-46);
- Jesus' statement, *If you love me you will keep my commandments.* (John 14:15);
- the First Letter of John which states, *Those who say, 'I love God', and hate their brothers or sisters, are liars; for those who do not love*

a brother or sister whom they have seen, cannot love God whom they have not seen. (1 John 4:20); and,

- the exhortation by Moses to God's people, *I call heaven and earth to witness against you today that I have set before you life and death, blessings and curses. Choose life so that you and your descendants may live, loving the LORD your God, obeying him, and holding fast to him; for that means life to you and length of days.* (Deut. 30:19-20).

What is sin?

In its essence, sin is a refusal or failure to observe the Greatest Commandment, which requires us to love God and to love our neighbour. So, at its heart, sin always involves a failure to love, or a lack of love in our attitudes or actions. In this way, sin invariably alienates us from God or from each other, or even from creation, and also reveals an unloving heart. Sin therefore breaks relationships: with God, with others, and with our environment. Consequently sin damages souls, especially our own.

The Catholic Catechism (July 2000) definition of sin includes the following:

> Sin is an offense against reason, truth, and right conscience; it is failure in genuine love for God and neighbour caused by a perverse attachment to certain goods. It wounds the nature of man and injures human solidarity. Sin is an offense against God. Sin sets itself against God's love for us and turns our hearts away from it. Like the first sin, it is disobedience, a revolt against God through the will to become *like gods*, knowing and determining good and evil. Sin is thus *love of oneself even to contempt of God.* (From 1849 and 1850)

Most people seem to know when they have done something wrong or are living in a state of sin; we all have a **conscience** that nags us and doesn't let us forget. If we have any doubts, then we also have St. Paul's checklist of the *fruits of sin or of self-indulgence* to help us assess the real state we are in, *fornication, impurity, licentiousness, idolatry, sorcery, enmities, strife, jealousy, anger, quarrels, dissensions, factions, envy, drunkenness, carousing, and things like these. I am warning you, as I warned you before: those who do such things will not inherit the kingdom of God* (Gal 5:19-21).

A *note of caution*—this list should be considered more like an Executive Summary, indicative rather than a comprehensive listing of all possible sins.

St. Paul also wrote, *all have sinned and fall short of the glory of God,* (Romans 3:23) and one can take a snapshot of the world—of humanity at any stage of its history—and find ample proof that his assertion is spot on. I know I am not, and I have yet to meet, someone who is perfect, who has no weaknesses or character defects. Yes, there can be very, very good, even inspirational people. Pope Francis might be considered to be in this category by many but even he has freely admitted on many occasions that he is first and foremost a sinner:

> I am a sinner ... I am sure of this. I am a sinner whom the Lord looked upon with mercy. I am, as I said to detainees in Bolivia, a forgiven man ... I still make mistakes and commit sins, and I confess every fifteen or twenty days. And if I confess it is because I need to feel that God's mercy is still upon me.[24]

Can we admit, together with Pope Francis, that we are sinners through and through?

Can we admit the same about ourselves? Sin certainly exists within the Church considered as the *people of God*.

Sin in the Church

Sin has been rife within our Church from its earliest days in the first century. In recent decades, as we all know only too well, the horrendous abuse of children and other vulnerable people has caused

---

24   Quoted in *National Catholic Reporter* 25th July 2016

untold damage to countless lives as well as to the mission with which our Church has been entrusted by Christ himself: to proclaim the Good News of *salvation* to all humankind. As an institution—and through the actions of a minority of priests as well as some bishops—the Church has seriously damaged itself in the public mindset, and in the marketplace of faith or belief systems to which people might be attracted or repelled. In relation to the latter, a possible indicator could well be an analysis of 2011 census data which suggested that, in Australia, approximately 20,000 people per year across all age groups are ceasing to identify as Catholic.[25]

Of course, the scandal of child abuse, and the inadequate response by the Church over decades, is not the only challenge for a Church alienating its members. An entrenched culture of clericalism, with an associated lack of accountability, openness or transparency in decision making, and the lack of inclusion of women, are all indicative of a Church operating in ways which are counter-cultural for all the wrong reasons. Some might even consider such institutional behaviours as inherently sinful, undermining the essence of the Gospel which Jesus preached.

And yet, *and yet* ... if anyone cares to look—and it doesn't need Sherlock Holmes' detective skills—one will find that there are a large number of Catholic people, as well as parish and school communities nevertheless striving to authentically live this Gospel. We can also find inspiring examples of engagement with, and support of, the broader community through agencies such as the Society of St. Vincent de Paul, Centacare, Rosies and the like, often assisting those who are most vulnerable and on the fringes of society, irrespective of beliefs. This is the very best of Christianity in action. At this level, the Church—as the people of God rather than as a bureaucratic institution—continues to

---

25 Dixon, R. & Reid, S. (2013). The Contemporary Catholic Community: A View from the 2011 Census. *The Australiasian Catholic Record* (90), 131-146

reveal the love of Christ in specific local contexts; *to make Jesus real*. However, such lived witness to the Gospel is almost totally out of the public eye; not at all newsworthy as far as the media is concerned.

So the light of Christ keeps on piercing the darkness or shadows of our Church if anyone cares to look.

Where are you able to see the light of Christ piercing the darkness, or trying to: whether this is in your own circumstances, in your family, at work, in your community, or in the Church?

In 1974, Carlo Carretto wrote the following which seems to go to the heart of the matter:

> How baffling you are, oh Church, and yet how I love you!
>
> How you have made me suffer, and yet how much I owe you!
>
> I should like to see you destroyed, and yet I need your presence.
>
> You have given me so much scandal and yet you have made me understand sanctity.
>
> I have seen nothing in the world more devoted to obscurity, more compromised, more false, and I have touched nothing more pure, more generous, more beautiful. How often I have wanted to shut the doors of my soul in your face, and how often I have prayed to die in the safety of your arms.
>
> No, I cannot free myself from you, because I am you, although not completely.
>
> And where should I go?[26]

Indeed! He goes on to write, *The Church's credibility is in the fact that notwithstanding 2000 years of sins committed by her personnel, she has preserved the faith, that this morning I saw one of her priests say over the bread, 'This is my body', and I received the Holy Communion of my master, the Lord Jesus.*[27]

So, just like none of us has ever met, or will ever meet, the perfect person, those who look for or expect perfection in the Church—or in its

---

26   Carretto, Carlo (1974). *The God who Comes*. London: Darton, Longman, Todd. p183

27   Ibid p189

If you are a 'bushed Catholic' or someone who has intentionally left the Church, might you have 'thrown out the baby with the bathwater'? Have you explored other spiritual pathways which might nurture your soul and spirituality, pathways that have been proven over the centuries and are Christian at their very core or essence?

clergy or its structure and processes—are very much searching in the wrong places, and unrealistically so at that! The Church always has been and always will be, the *broken Body of Christ*, a horde of sinners through and through, from top to bottom, and in all places where the Church is present.

This is very important to recognise and accept because people sometimes leave the Church, and in essence 'throw the baby out with the bathwater' because of something it, or someone in authority, has done. Of course, this is often very understandable especially when a person has been seriously hurt or damaged by—or through—the Church, as in the case of victims of child abuse or their families and friends.

However, in other situations, a perceived failure in the Church might sometimes be used as a convenient excuse (Just what I was looking for!) for some people to disengage from the challenge of reflecting more deeply, seeking what might give their lives direction and real meaning, a richer spiritual foundation. Perhaps they are also afraid of losing their independence and personal freedom by becoming, or remaining, part of a Church community. I know about this because I was once in such a place myself. When I now see other people do the same thing, it always makes me sad because the Church still possesses unmatchable spiritual treasures which they will never find because they have essentially shut the doors of their hearts, their minds and thus, their very souls.

Forgiveness: at the very Heart of Christianity

In a preceding chapter on the Christian revelation of God, we highlighted our faith in God's unconditional love, a love which cannot

'Forgive them Father for they know not what they are doing' (Luke 23 :34)

be earned but is always there for us to receive. This was profoundly illustrated by Jesus in his depiction of the father in the parable of the Prodigal Son (see Christian Revelation of God). God did not make humankind to be perfect, but instead gave us free will and thus enabled us to make choices, both good and bad.

Can we see that to do otherwise—to give humankind *no* free will— would essentially make us all like computers, robots, or apps? Start them up and have them run just as they are programmed! Unlike we humans, robots and apps are soul-less (or heartless) and are incapable of love.

Unlike robots and apps, and the like, which are often identical products of large production lines, each human being is a 'one-off', a unique creation. There is no one just like you or just like me that has ever lived on earth or will ever in the future. Each of us is therefore capable of entering into our own, unique, loving relationships with God and with others.

God took a great risk loving humankind into existence, out of a desire to share with us the overflowing love of the Trinity, hoping that we would freely choose not only to love God in return, but also to love each other as well. In doing so, God knew that we would all fail in this through making bad, or even very bad, choices. Fortunately for us, though, God also provided pathways for extending forgiveness and mercy, with the ultimate pathway revealed in and through Jesus Christ, God's beloved Son.

In order to receive God's forgiveness for our sins—or failures to love—only three things are necessary: a genuine sorrow for what we have done (not because we have got caught), a heartfelt desire to change our ways (the real meaning of repentance) and, very importantly, that we also forgive others for what they have done to us. The Lord's Prayer that Jesus taught makes this very clear, *Forgive us our trespasses as we forgive those who trespass against us*. It's a pre-condition: if we humbly approach God and ask forgiveness for ourselves, it will only be extended if we also have forgiven those who have caused us pain and hurt, or otherwise have offended us. Jesus illustrated this very clearly in the Parable of the Unforgiving Servant, see Matthew 18:23-35.

Christians are called to be people who epitomise forgiveness both in the giving and receiving, and to model this for our modern world, in which a lack of ability to forgive seems, at times, to be endemic. The inherent wisdom of this is evident in many pastoral situations I have encountered. Un-forgiveness can eat away at a person's insides like a cancer and wreck the lives of others where long-held grudges, deep hurts and unresolved conflicts are carried (even nurtured) like so much excess baggage, weighing people down for years, sometimes even decades. Forgiving hearts can radically set people free leading them into pathways of mercy and compassion, just as they might be hoping that God will be merciful and compassionate with them. Hopefully, you, the reader, will also have well and truly discovered the healing power of forgiveness for yourself.

Just a final note—whilst forgiveness is something that we can extend without the cooperation of anyone else, *reconciliation* (implying a settlement or resolution) does require such willingness and cooperation by others.

> *Can you think of an example of where your act of forgiveness has really set you free?*

This will not always be possible or practicable. For example, a person who has offended or hurt us may have died, or may not be interested. In this case, it is nevertheless important that we extend forgiveness from our hearts anyway.

God is always waiting for us to do this ... and then, and only then, can we can ask for forgiveness from God, trusting always in God's merciful love and compassion.

Of course, with God, reconciliation is freely offered to us 24x7!

Summary

This chapter has sought to remind us of the reality of sin, and the proper place of forgiveness and mercy at the very heart of Christianity. These matters are not only core to our personal authenticity as Christians, but are also central to the well-being of our church as the people of God, and indeed they underpin what seems to be so needed amongst human kind; tolerance and acceptance of one another as people who are all less than perfect. If we have not really grasped the central importance and power of forgiveness, then we might easily find ourselves in very dark places, including those of our own making, because of our unforgiving hearts.

Gathered around a kitchen or dining room table as the focal point for home prayer and liturgies: being church in the outback.

SOME GUIDELINES FOR PRAYER AND DIY LITURGIES

Background

Lord, teach us how to pray (Luke 11: 1), was a request of Jesus by his first followers and, in many ways, it is a question that continues to be asked today by those who sincerely wish to follow in His footsteps as modern-day disciples. We know that Jesus responded to the question by teaching them the Lord's Prayer which is still widely known and prayed today. Now, however, there are countless ways to pray as well as books and websites full of prayers, including a very large list of specifically Catholic prayers. Many readers will be familiar with at least some of these, which will be referenced in this chapter.

In addition, however—and this is important especially for Catholic families and communities in the bush—liturgies are also available for regular use on the stations, or in the towns when families, friends or communities gather for a special occasion, such as Christmas or Easter, or for Sunday worship, when no Priest (or Deacon or Religious) is available. Many bush Catholics have become accustomed to gather together and worship only 'when Father comes around'. Consequently, many have become used to a *liturgical* diet bordering on *starvation*! This doesn't have to—and perhaps can't—continue as the normality of the future. This chapter, therefore, includes some guidance and possible liturgy templates for family or community gatherings. On such occasions, Christ is present through the Word of Sacred Scripture and in keeping with His promise, *For where two or three are gathered in my name, I am there among them.*(Matt 18:20)

Families with young children, concerned about forming them more fully into spiritually mature Catholics, might especially like to consider inclusion of family prayer times and liturgies into their daily/weekly lives. This may require planning and setting aside special times in what are likely to be already busy schedules. It is never easy to be disciplined in prayer!

Personal Prayer

The importance of any of our relationships is always very clearly demonstrated by the time and effort we commit to them, which indicates the space we have made for them in our souls. So it is with God. If we call ourselves Christian but rarely, if ever, set aside any time for prayer, to waste time with God, could it be that we are just kidding ourselves? In reflecting on

> *What priority do you currently place on prayer?*
>
> *What does this say about your relationship with God?*
>
> *Can you be more disciplined in setting aside a regular time and special place for prayer?*

the Rule of Benedict, Sr Joan Chittister, osb, writes:

> The stress on our responsibility to call ourselves to prayer is an insight as fresh for the twenty first century as it was for the sixth. For all of us, prayer must be regular, not haphazard, nor erratic nor chance. At the same time, it cannot be routine or meaningless or without substance. Prayer must bring beauty, substance and structure to our otherwise chaotic and superficial lives or life itself becomes chaotic and superficial. A life of spiritual substance is a life of quality.[28]

In addition, while some might argue that because God is everywhere, we can also pray anywhere, proven experience over many

---

28   Chittister, Joan osb. (1992) *The Rule of Benedict–Insight for the Ages*. New York: Crosssroad. P131-2

centuries is very clear—it is very important that all who wish to relate more and more fully and deeply with the Living God must have at least *one space or place* where we can go to be about nothing else but spending time with God in prayer. Then from *that* place or space, we can then take the Presence of God into every other space of our lives.

So our prayer life needs to be **intentional**, in both time and space and in an ongoing commitment. Is anything more important than spending time with God alone?

After setting aside a regular time and a space for our prayer, what next? Well, there are many different ways to pray, and opportunities to find a way that you find helpful and life-giving for yourself. Some people like to use formal or set prayers and there are any number of these (for example you might like to search for *Catholic Prayers* on Google, or try one of the links below.)

Others like to spend time praying with Scripture by reading a section of the Bible and then prayerfully reflecting on how the text applies to their lives. (A more formal technique for this is *Lectio Divina* which was described in the earlier chapter on the Bible).

There is also a wonderful app (**Universalis**), suitable for both iPhone and Android devices. This app is available for approximately $20 and has the Daily Readings for Mass, the Daily Office, Lectio Divina guidelines for each day, and much more. It can be used offline. The beauty of this app is that it replaces books which collectively weigh several kilos and cost hundreds of dollars, and provides all the information in a convenient and accessible format.

We have already considered *meditative or contemplative* styles of prayer in a previous chapter.

Finally, many people use a number of different styles of prayer, sometimes incorporating music and art to enrich the experience. What prayer styles you use is completely up to you personally ... but pray we must!

Family or Community (DIY) Liturgies

As well as individual prayer, real possibilities exist—as indicated above—for families or local communities to gather for liturgies, either on Sundays in order to keep a regular day for gathering to worship and keeping the Sabbath holy, or for special occasions including but not limited to:

- religious feasts (like Easter and Christmas),
- national days (such as Australia Day and Anzac Day),
- significant local events, and,
- family celebrations (such as anniversaries and significant birthdays).

> *Can you accept that organising or leading a liturgy for your family would primarily be an act of service for them?*
>
> *Or would you perhaps be overly concerned about not doing it properly?*
>
> *Do you think Jesus would care if you did your best but made some mistakes?*

Importantly, while families—and, say, any station workers—are able to gather and do so relatively informally as long as someone is prepared to organise and lead any liturgy, caution is needed for more public or communal liturgies which are more formal and therefore ought to be done well. This applies especially to regular Sunday liturgies of the Word and/or Communion without a priest or deacon and held in a church.

In that case, Lay Leaders of Liturgy are trained and formally appointed by the Priest or Parish Pastoral Leader to lead such services on a regular basis.

For ease of reference and use, the following liturgies have been included in the appendices:

Appendix A: Liturgy of the Word

Appendix B: Australia Day Liturgy (suitable for ecumenical use)

Appendix C: Christmas Day Liturgy (suitable for ecumenical use)

Appendix D: Easter Liturgy – Some Suggestions

Appendix E: Praying with the Dying

Further liturgies can of course be developed. The appendices are provided as practical resources which can be used immediately as well as to indicate what might be possible for other circumstances. Importantly, and as already stated, you don't have to wait until a priest or a Mass is available to pray or worship together with your family, co-workers, friends or community members.

It's up to each one of us whether we wish to remain on any starvation diets as far as liturgical worship is concerned ... why don't you take the lead? Your Priest, Deacon or Religious would be delighted to help you!

Some Useful Resources

Catholic Prayers: Here are some of many possible web links:
http://www.beginningcatholic.com/catholic-prayers
https://www.yourcatholicguide.com/
http://www.catholicity.com/prayer/prayers.html

Daily Scripture Readings for the Mass: http://melbournecatholic.org.au/Daily-Readings

Daily Gospel Reflections: https://catholic-daily-reflections.com/daily-reflections/

Daily Audio Recordings of the Mass Readings: http://www.usccb.org/bible/readings-audio.cfm

Daily Video (YouTube) Reflections on the Daily Mass Readings, produced by the US Catholic Bishops Commission: http://www.usccb.org/bible/reflections/index.cfm

Lenten Programs: These are produced annually by several Archdiocese and Diocese in Australia. You may wish to seek advice from your clergy or Religious.

Capturing well recognised symbols of Catholic belief and practice through the Sacraments.

Mustering the Sacraments and Other Rituals: Practical Aspects

Overview

One of the distinguishing features of Catholic faith and belief is the emphasis placed on the Sacraments, a word that is not often heard these days. In essence, the Sacraments signify and make present God's loving involvement at key stages of our lives. Each sacrament is also based on some aspect of the teachings of Jesus and in that context can be connected to one or more specific scripture texts.

In the early 1960s the Second Vatican Council summed up the purpose of the sacraments as follows, *to sanctify people, to build up the body of Christ and to give worship to God ... they are signs [to] nourish, strengthen and express [our faith]* (Constitution on the Liturgy 59). Sacraments thus unite us more closely with God and to the Church—viewed as the people of God—at key stages of our lives and they do so by using everyday materials such as water, wine, bread, fire and oil to remind us that God is fully present to us in our humanity. The sacraments have both a human and divine aspect to them.

There are seven sacraments in all: three **sacraments of initiation** (Baptism, Confirmation and Communion), two **sacraments of healing** (Reconciliation and Anointing) and two **sacraments of** service (Marriage and Holy Orders). In this chapter, we will briefly describe each one and then look at some practical aspects of receiving these 'out in the bush' ... except for Holy Orders which is usually celebrated only in the Diocesan cathedral or a large church.

It is important to note that the discussion below refers to the Sacraments of Initiation separately as applying to babies and young children. For older children and for adults, after a suitable period of preparation and formation, the three Sacraments of Initiation are usually received together. For more information about this, please ask your Priest, Deacon or Religious.

Baptism, Christening or 'Wetting the Baby's Head'

From the very earliest days of the Church in the first century, baptism has been the consistent sign and symbol of a person becoming a Christian. It's a tradition that is nearly 2,000 years old, and there are not many such traditions! When we baptise someone within the Catholic Church, usually a little baby or child, we use the symbolism of lighting their candle from the Easter candle as a concrete sign of their receiving the Christian faith handed down in a similar way to an Olympic torch relay, with each runner receiving, then carrying and ultimately passing on the flame.

Water, however, is the primary symbol of baptism signifying life and purification. In Baptism, we become a new creation, a child of God and a member of His Church on earth. We ask God to remove from the person being baptised the effects of sin in our world and to give him/her the graces needed, not only to grow as Christians, but also to actively exercise their baptismal vocation by sharing in the mission which Jesus entrusted to his church.

Now for some practical aspects:

- **Timing:** Given that the baptism of a baby or young child is also a wonderful occasion for families and friends to gather in celebration, this often means that there can be a lengthy delay in organising a time and place when everyone can come together, let alone organising a minister. When selecting a date, please ensure that you contact the minister (priest, deacon or sister) who you would like to perform the baptism *as early as possible*. This is especially important if significant travel is involved and avoids the embarrassment of having all your family and friends organised for the day and time and then finding out no one is available to perform the baptism. Yes, it has happened before.

- **Place:** While a church is still the normal and preferred place for a baptism ceremony, this is not always practicable in more remote areas, so baptisms have been performed in places such as cattle station homesteads, or private homes, and sometimes in a creek or river.

- **Preparation:** Normally the person whom you have contacted to perform the baptism will also assist in preparing you, and if old enough, your child. This could involve some preparation sessions, face to face or over the phone/Skype, as well as working through some booklets or similar reading material.

Importantly, one of the first questions you will be asked to respond to at the commencement of the baptism ceremony, essentially invites you to confirm publicly that you fully understand your commitment to raise your child as a Catholic. Consequently, to be able to answer this question truly and honestly, you might need to consider and discuss beforehand what this might look like in your particular family circumstances. For example, it might be through praying together regularly, or reading your child Bible stories when they are old enough, or eventually sending your child to a Catholic school, or a combination of these and other activities.

In selecting godparents for your child, please be aware that *at least one of them needs to be Catholic, ideally a practising Catholic*. Godparents will also be 'put on the spot', as it were, by being asked to make a public commitment to help parents in raising the child as a Catholic. Once again, it would be good if godparents reflect beforehand on what this commitment might look like for them in practice.

Finally, before the day of the baptism, parents need to organise a baptismal candle for their child and a white garment (shirt or dress) to signify their becoming a new and pure creation as a Christian.

- **Selecting a Spot:** Ideally the chosen spot—if not in a church—will provide some shade and protection from breezes or wind as well as allowing the gathering to not only see but also participate as much (or as little) as they would like.

- **During the Baptism:** Sometimes in bush Christenings, the party has started well beforehand (you know what I mean). So just before the ceremony begins, please ask all your family and friends to finish their drinks as a sign of respect for what is about to occur.

- **After the Baptism:** The baptism of your child will be entered into the Baptism Register of the parish within the geographical boundaries of which the baptism took place. So, if for example you live in the Gulf Savannah Parish, but your child is baptised, say, in Mareeba, then it will be recorded in the Mareeba Parish Baptism Register. You will be given a Baptismal Certificate to keep as a record.

- **Baptism in a Crisis (or similar situation):** While the ordinary minister for the Sacrament of Baptism is a bishop, priest or deacon, the Catholic Church also makes provisions for where there is some sort of crisis or other contingency (for example if a child becomes very seriously ill and such ministers are not available) where anyone can administer this Sacrament (Canon 1256). However, this exact wording must be used:

(Name) *I baptise you in the name of the Father, and of the Son and of the Holy Spirit*

If such a baptism is performed, and if practicable, the respective parish office should be informed so that the baptism can be recorded.

Confirmation

As we need assistance growing and maturing in our physical and social lives, so the Sacrament of Confirmation assists us we start to mature in the faith by releasing in us the *gifts* of the Holy Spirit, namely: wisdom, understanding, counsel, fortitude, knowledge, piety (or holiness) and fear of the Lord. This last one is not about being afraid of God, but recognises our true standing before our Creator, and that, *our good lies in humble, respectful and trusting self-abandonment into his hands. This is fear of the Lord: abandonment in the goodness of our Father who loves us so much.*[29]

St. Paul writes about the *fruits* of the Spirit which reveal the Holy Spirit being present in us, and in the way we connect with others and indeed the world around us. These fruits are: love, joy, peace, patience, kindness, generosity, faithfulness, gentleness and self-control (Galatians 5:22-23). (You might note that in this letter, these fruits are held in stark contrast with the fruits of self-indulgence—covered above in the chapter about sin and forgiveness.)

For many older Catholics, Confirmation was received when they were entering into their teens. However, in recent years, there has been a widespread move to restore this Sacrament in its proper order as a Sacrament of Initiation; namely after Baptism but before Eucharist

---

29   Pope Francis, General Audience, St. Peter's Square, 11 June 2014

(or Communion). This is now the practice in the Diocese of Cairns, and in other Diocese throughout Australia. Consequently, for most Catholic children, Confirmation now occurs in their lower primary years, followed at a later stage, but still in lower primary, by their First Communions.

The Sacrament of Confirmation is normally administered by the Bishop, however, priests are sometimes delegated to do this when numbers (or distances) are too large for the Bishop to reasonably do so. Children are prepared for Confirmation—and indeed for Reconciliation and Eucharist—in a number of ways. If they attend a Catholic school, sacramental preparation programs are undertaken either by the school or parish. For Catholic families in the bush, special arrangements are generally made for appropriate preparation sessions either in person, for example by a Religious or Deacon—face to face or via internet technologies such as Skype—or through sending suitable material that can be used by parents to instruct their children.

Confirmation schedules are usually planned early in each calendar year. Given the special challenges of the bush, it is wise to plan well ahead and ensure that your desire to have your child or children confirmed is taken into account. Depending on local circumstances, Confirmation can be received either in a special liturgy or during a scheduled Mass.

Details of all confirmations are also entered into the registers of the Parish in which they take place.

Eucharist and First Communion

The centrality and importance of the Eucharist for sustaining and nurturing the Catholic faith has already been considered above so will not be repeated here. When any person receives the Eucharist for the first time (First Communion), it signifies their becoming full members of the worldwide Catholic *community*, also referred to as the

Body of Christ. In that sense, *Communion* is actually inseparable from *community*, i.e. a group of people gathered together as one, in faith, to worship God in, with, and through the person of Jesus Christ.

First Communion is usually administered by a priest during a scheduled Mass and many families still choose to celebrate afterwards to mark this special occasion in the life of their child/children.

Appropriate preparation of children is usually undertaken in a similar way to Confirmation. Once again, as much as notice as is possible should be provided.

Reconciliation (or Confession)

As we have already noted in the discussion on sin, due to our human weakness and imperfection, we often do not live up to our dignity as sons and daughters of God, perhaps being better described as *sinners through and through*. In our church, the Sacrament of Reconciliation celebrates the forgiveness and mercy of God as we humbly acknowledge and confess our sins.

Children are generally introduced to this sacrament at about the time that they are able to distinguish right from wrong. After suitable preparation, they are then invited to make their first reconciliation or confession to a priest.

While all Catholics are encouraged to receive this Sacrament regularly, many if not most Catholics do not do so. Certainly, for those living in remote areas, access to a priest for hearing one's confession, can be very difficult to coordinate and arrange. Importantly then, when we realize we have sinned, and irrespective of how far it is to the nearest confessional, we can approach God directly in sorrow for what we have done, ask for His mercy and forgiveness, and make a genuine commitment to not sin again.

If the sin is a very serious one, the Church teaches that we must go to confession as soon as possible. There are very good reasons for this—telling another person confidentially about what we have done can release the burden of keeping it all secret eating away at our very souls. It is healing to actually hear the words of absolution, *I absolve you from your sins*, from the priest who is representing God for us.

Even without any serious sins, a regular confession is a sound spiritual practice, a 'tune-up', much like having our cars serviced regularly to keep them in good running order. So, when is the next time you might enter into the Sacrament of Reconciliation?

Holy Orders & the Permanent Deacon

Christ did not leave the Church without a sacrament of leadership and service. God raises up Deacons, Priests, and Bishops to serve, lead, and govern the Church as a community of faith, and commissions these through the various levels of the Sacrament of Holy Orders.

While Catholics are very familiar with the roles and functions of Bishops and Priests, and some may have encountered Deacons placed in parishes before they are ordained as Priests, the role and functions of Permanent Deacons (of which I am one) are not well understood. Unlike Bishops and Parish Priests whose responsibilities are reasonably consistent and uniform across the Catholic Church throughout the world, the roles and responsibilities of Permanent Deacons are many and varied.

In 2015, there were some 43,000 Permanent Deacons throughout the world. In our Diocese of Cairns, there are currently seven Deacons, six married with families and one single man. The way we each exercise our diaconal vocations is very different, depending on the various circumstances we find ourselves in, and on the gifts we have each been given. Some are in the full time employ of the Diocese, others in secular or other employment. However, there are some basics which are common to all of us:

- We have been ordained for service within the Diocese of Cairns which means that we are likely to remain here for some time.
- While we are in Holy Orders, we are not mini priests ... nor lay people.
- Permanent Deacons do have liturgical roles such as: assisting at Mass (especially by proclaiming the Gospel and as the ordinary minister of the chalice), leading liturgies of the Word and/or Communion in the absence of a priest, and presiding at Baptisms, Weddings and Funerals. However, none of these are our main charism as Deacons which is to serve the people of God when they are not gathered for worship or liturgies.
- While a priest comes into his own, as it were, when Catholics gather together, the Permanent Deacon's charism is (or should be) most manifest in serving a community when it is dispersed and engaged in everyday matters, including of course the everyday living of their faith. The ways of serving a community will vary depending on the particular situation of that community and the particular gifts and circumstances of the Deacon. Ideally, with the guidance of the Holy Spirit, the **greatest** *need* of the community will match the **greatest** *desire* of the Deacon and thus enable him to serve in ways that are Christ centered and are life giving for all concerned.

More information on the Permanent Diaconate in Australia can be found at the following link: https://www.catholic.org.au/acbc-media/downloads/bishops-commissions/bishops-commission-for-church-ministry-1/1864-norms-for-the-formation-of-permanent-deacons-and-guidelines-for-the-ministry-and-life-of-permanent-deacons/file

Or just ask a Deacon!

Interestingly, in August 2016, Pope Francis established a commission to investigate the possibility of women being restored to the diaconate. They were present within the church during the first centuries of its existence, although perhaps not in quite the same way as today's Permanent Diaconate. So, watch this space!

Marriage

The Sacrament of Marriage celebrates the human capacity for love and total commitment, and also serves as a witness to Christ's love for the Church (which St. Paul, in particular, compares to married love). Marriage involves all aspects of life: mental, physical and spiritual. While beginning with a wedding service in the presence of God and the faith community, a husband and wife continue to confer the Sacrament on one another whenever they offer themselves in the service of the other and the larger community. Thus, marriage is an ongoing sacrament.

That said, there are just too many possible practical situations and issues all based in widely varying individual circumstances, to cover in this brief guide. If you have fallen in love and would like to enter into marriage in and through the Catholic Church, the best advice that can be given is to contact your priest or deacon as early as possible. This will enable you to discuss your particular circumstances, work out whether you are able to marry according to the rites of the Catholic Church, get the necessary paperwork started—both under the Australian Marriage Act and as required by the Church—and to start planning for the big day.

Anointing of the Sick

Previously called the Last Rites or Extreme Unction, administered when people were approaching death, the Sacrament of Anointing is now also used for when people are sick or injured in any way, whether in body, mind or spirit. Sometimes we pray in and through this

Sacrament of Anointing that the person will be restored to full health, and at other times, we pray that it will prepare someone to accept and prepare for the reality of death.

A priest administers the Sacrament of Anointing and this can be requested either directly if you know the priest, or indirectly if, for example, you have a loved one seriously ill or dying in hospital. The staff will usually be able to assist in contacting one of the local priests or the hospital chaplain.

In addition, communion can be brought to those who are sick by a priest, deacon or suitably trained lay person.

When someone is seriously ill or dying in a remote area, and there is no priest available to administer the Sacrament of Anointing, there is nevertheless a range of simple prayer liturgies that can bring spiritual comfort to the sick or dying person, to pray for God's mercy and forgiveness for any sins that they may have committed and to spiritually support those caring for them. Appendix E is one possible liturgy for these situations.

Bush Funerals

While the experience of most Catholics is that funerals are normally undertaken by a priest, this is not essential. Deacons, Religious or lay people can conduct Catholic funerals if no priest is available. Of course, for a lay person without any experience or training, this can be a very daunting task.

For Catholics living in rural and remote areas, a lay-led funeral may sometimes be the only option available due to combined circumstances of distance and lack of available *professionals* (Priests, Religious or Deacons). If you find yourself in such a situation, as well as possibly being quite confronting, it is also a great honour to perform this service on behalf of a family member, or friend, or community member.

I could not resist including this photo of the sign at the entrance gate for the Normanton Cemetery saying 'No Camping –on the spot fines apply'. Presumably longer stays are OK?

People who will be able to assist you include:

- Your local council staff, to organise any venues and preparation of the gravesite if a burial is to take place,
- The funeral director, and,
- A Priest, Deacon or Religious—even if not available to preside at the funeral, they will be able to greatly assist you in planning a dignified funeral service for your loved one.

Normally, the funeral director would ask the family, in conjunction with the presider, to organise the order of the funeral service by selecting hymns, readings, prayers and so on. Families also usually prepare a little booklet with the order of service included, generally with some photos of their loved one. This enables all those attending to follow the order of the funeral service and participate as appropriate and gives them a memorial booklet to retain. Eulogies can also be included in these booklets, as well as reflective poems or verses. The design and contents of such booklets vary widely—as they should—because every person and family is unique.

Of course, if the family (or deceased) requests a Funeral Mass, then there is no real option other than to try and secure the services of a priest. In this case, there may have to be some greater flexibility in timing which may lead to a longer delay for the funeral to take place.

If you do find yourself leading a Catholic funeral somewhere 'out in the bush', please remember to advise the Parish Priest or Administrator *of the parish in which the funeral takes place* so that the details of the deceased can be entered into the parish register.

Summary

This Chapter has sought to provide a brief overview of each of the seven Sacraments, focussing on some of the practical aspects of both preparation and administration of each of these in rural and remote contexts. If more information is needed, please contact your Parish Priest, Deacon or Religious.

Importantly, the more notice you can give of your desire to personally receive any of the Sacraments, or for a loved one to receive one of the Sacraments, the better chance of being able to do so in a timely manner—if not on the day of your choosing than on another suitable day.

Time to get going!

CONCLUSION

Well, this brings us to the end of this field guide. It certainly grew to something much larger than was originally expected, and yet I find myself asking, *Is it enough?* The answer can only be, *No!* At the same time, there is a need to stop writing, or reading, and start **doing** ...

In that sense, I sincerely hope and pray that this book may be of some use in suggesting some possible pathways into a deeper and richer personal faith founded very firmly on very fertile and proven spiritual traditions and practices. Many of these have ancient origins and have already helped countless numbers of people in their search for God or His Kingdom, or in letting God find them! May the disciplined application of some or all of these practices lead us all into deeper and life-giving encounters with the Living God, as revealed by Jesus the Christ.

As well as being useful for individuals, I hope that this book will also be family friendly. Each family is indeed called to be a little church revealing the Kingdom of God in its own unique circumstances. Understanding that *the Church is a family ... and a family is church* will, hopefully, uncover new ways of *being* Catholic every day, and not only when we are gathered together in a church building.

While this field guide has been especially written for isolated Catholics living in rural and remote areas, it might be useful in other contexts as well, as suggested in the Introduction.

In conclusion, I humbly offer this brief guide from a deep sense of solidarity with you all as my brothers and sisters in Christ. May He richly bless all of us as we seek deeper and richer relationships with Him and with one another.

God bless!

APPENDICES

Appendix A: Sunday or Holy Day Liturgy of the Word
Appendix B: Australia Day Liturgy (suitable for ecumenical use)
Appendix C: Christmas Day Liturgy (suitable for ecumenical use)
Appendix D: Easter Liturgy – Some Suggestions
Appendix E: Praying with the Dying

Please note: For ease of access and printing, copies of these appendices can be downloaded from the Diocese of Cairns website via this link:http://www.cairns.catholic.org.au/documents/bushedcatholics.html.

APPENDIX A
LITURGY OF THE WORD FOR
SUNDAYS AND HOLY DAYS

Introduction and Preparations

This Appendix contains a simplified liturgy which focusses on the Word of God made present in the Bible readings which the Church has chosen for a particular Sunday or Holy Day. This simple liturgy is designed to be used within families, or with friends or neighbours in informal settings at home, on stations, in a meeting room and so on. It is not designed—or approved—for use in public settings or in a church where more formal arrangements are necessary, also including Lay Leaders of Liturgy who have been officially trained and commissioned.

To prepare for this informal liturgy, you will need:

- some copies of this Appendix so that those attending can follow the liturgy and participate appropriately,
- copies of the Bible readings and Responsorial Psalm for that Sunday or Holy Day (these are available on line via the following link: http://melbournecatholic.org.au/Daily-Readings),
- (optional) a small table at the centre of the gathering covered with a white cloth and with a candle and a Bible open at the Gospel reading for the day, and,
- (optional) some sacred music suitable for quiet reflection and/or some well-known hymns to enable those present to sing along with an instrument (such as a piano) or with a CD.

The Liturgy

Gathering of the Community

Liturgical Greeting

The leader of prayer goes to the place from which he/she will preside.

Leader: In the name of the Father, and of the Son, and of the
Holy Spirit.

All: *Amen.*

Leader: Christ be with us, Christ within us,
Christ behind us, Christ before us,
Christ beside us, now and forever.

All: *Amen.*

Introductory Remarks

Leader: We have gathered here on this day to be nourished
by God's word, to pray together as Christians and to
worship our God. As we gather together and unite as
one, let us ask for the grace and presence of the Holy
Spirit to guide and bless our liturgy today.

Opening Rite

Litany of Praise

Leader: Our Saviour is rich in mercy and kindness. Let us now
acknowledge our sinfulness and ask for His mercy.

Leader: Jesus, Word of God, you came to reveal God's love to
us. Lord, have mercy.

All: *Lord, have mercy.*

Leader: Jesus, risen from the dead, you bring us to new life.
Christ, have mercy.

All: *Christ have mercy.*

Leader: Jesus, Son of Justice, you bring together the scattered flock of God. Lord, have mercy.

All: *Lord, have mercy.*

Leader: May Almighty God have mercy on us, forgive us our sins,and bring us to everlasting life.

All: *Amen.*

Opening Prayer

Leader: Let us pray (Pause). Heavenly Father, today we offer ourselves to you just as we are. We come together as your children with all our gifts as well as all our needs and we humbly ask for Your help and grace to grow more fully into the people You have created us to be. We ask this through Jesus Christ, Your Son, Our Lord.

All: *Amen.*

Liturgy of the Word

Leader: May the word of God always be heard in our lives, as it unfolds the mystery of Christ before us and achieves our salvation.

(Readings and responses are taken from the Readings of the day (previously downloaded or marked in a Bible if available). Different people might be invited to read the various readings or lead the Responsorial Psalm. There should be a short pause for reflection after each reading.)

First Reading

Responsorial Psalm

Second Reading*

Gospel

Reflections

After the Gospel is read, the Leader invites the gathering to reflect on the readings that they have just heard. When enough time has been allowed, the Leader then asks if anyone would like to comment on any of the readings, especially if they felt that a text was speaking into their particular situation or circumstances and if they would like to share that with others present. Alternatively, people may wish to share a particular insight that one of the readings has given them.

After any reflections are shared, a suitable sacred song or hymn might be sung/played if available.

Profession of Faith

Leader: In union with the whole Church, let us now profess
our faith.

All: *I believe in God,*
the Father almighty,
Creator of heaven and earth,
and in Jesus Christ, his only Son, our Lord,
who was conceived by the Holy Spirit,
born of the Virgin Mary,
suffered under Pontius Pilate,
was crucified, died and was buried;
he descended into hell;
on the third day he rose again from the dead;
he ascended into heaven,
and is seated at the right hand of God the Father almighty;
from there he will come to judge the living and the dead.

I believe in the Holy Spirit, the holy catholic Church,
the communion of saints, the forgiveness of sins, the
resurrection of the body, and life everlasting. Amen.

General Intercessions

Leader: In response to God's word proclaimed in our midst,
we pray to God for our needs, the needs of the
Church and the world.

The leader now invites everyone, if they wish, to pray for any specific intentions, such as for someone who is sick, for a son or daughter away from home, for the needs of the community and so on. When it seems appropriate the leader concludes with the following prayer:

> Leader; God of love, hear the prayers of your people and grant us today what we ask of you in faith.
>
> We ask this through Christ our Lord.
>
> *All:* Amen.

Proclamation of Praise

All may say or sing the Gloria. However this is not used during Advent and Lent.

> *All:* Glory to God in the highest,
> and on earth peace to people of good will.
> We praise you,
> we bless you,
> we adore you,
> we glorify you,
> we give you thanks for your great glory,
> Lord God, heavenly King,
> O God, almighty Father.
> Lord Jesus Christ, Only Begotten Son,
> Lord God, Lamb of God, Son of the Father,
> you take away the sins of the world, have mercy on us;
> you take away the sins of the world, receive our prayer;
> you are seated at the right hand of the Father, have mercy on us.
> For you alone are the Holy One,
> you alone are the Lord,
> you alone are the Most High,
> Jesus Christ,
> with the Holy Spirit,
> in the glory of God, the Father.
> Amen.

Sign of Peace

Leader: Let us seal our prayer with a gesture of unity and
reconciliation as we offer one another a sign of peace.
The sign of peace is exchanged in the usual manner.

Lord's Prayer

Leader: At the Saviour's command and formed by divine
teaching, we dare to say:

All: *Our Father, who art in heaven,*
hallowed be thy name.
Thy kingdom come.
Thy will be done on earth, as it is in heaven.
Give us this day our daily bread.
And forgive us our trespasses,
as we forgive those who trespass against us,
and lead us not into temptation,
but deliver us from evil.
For the kingdom, the power and the glory are yours,
now and forever. Amen.

Blessing

Leader: May the God of hope fill us with every joy in
believing.
May the peace of Christ abound in our hearts.
May the Holy Spirit enrich us with gifts for service,
now and forever

All: *Amen.*

Dismissal

Leader: Let us go in peace, glorifying the Lord by our life.
All: *Thanks be to God.*

APPENDIX B
AUSTRALIA DAY LITURGY

Gathering Song- a song of praise familiar to all may be sung here.

Greeting – leader/s welcome all present

Reader 1:

> In the early years of colonisation, explorers set off to discover something of this vast continent that we call home. They saw her beauty and her terror; from the seas, to the mountains, to the deserts.
>
> In our own times, we are all explorers on another journey of discovery. We are touching the beauty and the terror that lies within the vastness of our psyche. The reality of terrorism so close to our shores, years of drought, climatic changes and economic downturn, the growth of cities, an increased awareness of the plight of the refugees and asylum seekers, the growth of multiculturalism, and an appreciation of living in this land of peace and plenty. Today we stand together to ask God's blessing on this great nation of ours:
>
> on the land and on her peoples;

those who live in the city and those who live in the country;
those who were born here;
and those who have come from afar ...

Call to Prayer

Leader: Let us pray ...

Leader: This land reflects your face, O God

Ever ancient, always new.

All: Give praise in God's holy place.

Leader: This land sounds with your voice, O God
        – Calling for justice and tolerance.

All: Give praise in God's holy place.

Leader: This land breathes with your life, O God
        – The spirit alive in the people.

All: Give praise in God's holy place.

(A large prominent candle is lit)

Act of Penitence

Leader: Though Christ has called us into one body, the oneness
        of the peoples of this land has been broken by acts of
        oppression and the failure of compassion.

Pause for silence

Let us therefore acknowledge our brokenness, confident
in God's power and promise to make us whole.

Leader: Lord have mercy,

All: Lord have mercy.

Leader: Christ have mercy,

All: Christ have mercy.

Leader: Lord have mercy.

All: Lord have mercy.

Opening Prayer

Leader: Bounteous God,

We give thanks for this ancient and beautiful land,

a land of despair and hope,

a land of wealth and abundant harvests,

a land of fire, drought and flood.

We pray that your Spirit may continue to move in this land,

and bring forgiveness, reconciliation, and an end to all

injustice.

We make this prayer through Jesus Christ our Lord.

All: *Amen*

The Word of God

First Reading:

A reading from the prophet Isaiah (32:15-18)

(The effect of justice will be peace.)

Once more there will be poured on us the spirit from above; then shall the wilderness be fertile land; and fertile land become forest.

In the wilderness justice will come to live and integrity in the fertile land; integrity will bring peace, justice give lasting security.

My people will live in a peaceful home, in safe houses, in quiet dwellings.

This is the word of the Lord.

All: *Thanks be to God.*

Psalm   [If not sung, read side to side] (84:9-14)

Antiphon: The Lord speaks of peace to his people.

Side 1: I will hear what the Lord God has to say, a voice that

speaks of peace. His help is near for those who fear him

and his glory will dwell in our land.

Side 2:   Mercy and faithfulness have met;
                           justice and peace have embraced.
                           Faithfulness shall spring up from the
                           earth and justice look down from heaven.

Side 1: The Lord will make us prosper and our earth shall yield
        its fruit. Justice shall march before him and peace shall
        follow his steps.

Antiphon: *The Lord speaks of peace to his people.*

Second Reading

A reading from the first letter of Paul to the Corinthians. (12:4-11)
(One and the same Spirit distributes different gifts as he chooses.)

There is a variety of gifts but always the same Spirit; there are all
sorts of service to be done, but always to the same Lord; working in
all sorts of different ways in different people, it is the same God who
is working in all of them. The particular way in which the Spirit is
given to each person is for a good purpose. One may have the gift of
preaching with wisdom given him by the Spirit; another may have
the gift of preaching instruction given him by the same Spirit; and
another the gift of faith given by the same Spirit; another again the
gift of healing, through this one Spirit; one, the power of miracles;
another, prophecy; another the gift of recognising spirits; another
the gift of tongues and another the ability to interpret them. All
these are the work of one and the same Spirit, who distributes
different gifts to different people just as he chooses.

This is the word of the Lord.

All: *Thanks be to God.*

Gospel Reading   (Matt 5:1-12)

A reading from the holy Gospel according to Matthew:

(*Rejoice and be glad, for your reward will be great in heaven.*) Jesus began to speak to the crowds. This is what he taught them:

How happy are the poor in spirit:
theirs is the kingdom of heaven.
Happy the gentle:
they shall have the earth for their heritage.
Happy those who mourn:
they shall be comforted.
Happy those who hunger and thirst for what is right:
they shall be satisfied.
Happy the merciful:
they shall have mercy shown them.
Happy the pure in heart:
they shall see God.
Happy the peacemakers:
they shall be called sons of God.
Happy those who are persecuted in the cause of right:
theirs is the kingdom of heaven.
Happy are you when people abuse you and persecute you and
speak all kinds of calumny against you on my account. Rejoice
and be glad, for your reward will be great in heaven.
This is the Gospel of the Lord.
Praise to you Lord Jesus Christ.
Reflection

... Silence ...

Song: *Lord of Earth and all His Creation* (TS 672, GA 554);
God of Peace (GA 553)

Affirmation of Faith

Leader: Let us now affirm our faith together as we pray:

All: *We believe in one God,*
         who made and loves all that is.
         We believe in Jesus Christ,
         God's only Son, our Lord,
         who was born, lived, died and rose again,
         and is coming to call all to account.
         We believe in the Holy Spirit,
         who calls, equips and sends out God's people,
         and brings all things to their true end.
         This is our faith, the faith of the Church: We believe in one
         God, Father, Son and Holy Spirit. Amen.

Intercessions

Leader: On this Australia Day, we place our petitions before
        the God of peace:

Reader 2: For the leaders of our country

All: *Lord of life, hear our prayer.*
         For peace between and among all peoples ....
         Lord of life, hear our prayer.
         For the unemployed, the homeless, the lonely of this
         land...
         Lord of life, hear our prayer.
         For all people who call Australia home... .
         Lord of life, hear our prayer.
         For the courage to be initiators of reconciliation ....
         Lord of life, hear our prayer.
         For the desire to work together to build our future
         Lord of *life, hear our prayer.*
         For eyes to see, ears to hear, and hearts to listen to each
         other.
         Lord of life, hear our prayer.
         For all who have lived and gifted Australia with their presence
         Lord of life, hear our prayer.

Our Father

Leader: Mindful of God's gracious bounty we pray

All: *Our Father in heaven,*
Hallowed be your name,
Your kingdom come,
Your will be done.
On earth as in heaven.

Give us today our daily bread.
Forgive us our sins
As we forgive those who sin against us.
Save us from the time of trial
And deliver us from evil.

For the kingdom, the power
And the glory are yours
Now and for ever. Amen.

Sign of Peace Leader (optional):

Leader:Brothers and Sisters,
Christ has reconciled us to God in one body by the cross.

All: *We meet in his name and share his peace.)*
Let us share the sign of peace.

Concluding Prayer:

Leader: Let us pray together:

All: *God of life,*
The wonders of our vast land
inspire and lead us to awe.
Enable us to see your shaping hand at work in all your gifts
to us.

Enlighten us,
that we may be able to bring our country and its people
to greater freedom and peace.
We make this our prayer,
through Christ your Son
Amen.

Blessing

Leader: May God enable us to be messengers of reconciliation.

All: Amen

Leader: May God enable us to be messengers of reconciliation.

All: Amen

Leader: May God bless our country and our people on this day.

All: Amen

Dismissal

Leader: Let us go forth in the peace of Christ Thanks be to God.

All: Amen

Song: Advance Australia Fair, or a familiar Song of Praise

APPENDIX C
CHRISTMAS LITURGY

Overview

This service has been developed by representatives from the Anglican, Catholic and Uniting Churches in Queensland. It is intended for use in a community or a family gathering where there is a desire to celebrate this very special day with Christian prayer and worship but where there is no priest or minister available. The service lends itself to have different prayers and readings shared by different people or, alternatively, it can be led by one person.

If not held in a church building, ideally the place of gathering should be around a specially prepared table or space, spread with a white cloth. The centre piece should ideally be a Bible which might be opened at one of the readings of this service. Other items that could be placed on the cloth might include one or two candles, a nativity scene (perhaps made previously by any children present), some flowers, and a cross. You might also consider including photos of those unable to be with you this Christmas for whatever reason.

Welcome [The leader or host welcomes everyone present.]

Leader/Reader: It's Christmas Day again! Perhaps today we can just spend a moment thinking about what the real meaning of

Christmas is. Some have had many Christmases, and others only a few. So, what does Christmas mean for you? Is it the gifts under the tree, the lights in the windows, the cards in the mail, big dinners with family and friends, stockings hanging in the living room, and greetings of *Merry Christmas* to those we meet? Is this really Christmas?

For many people, Christmas is a time of sorrow. They don't have the extra money to buy presents for their children, family, and friends. Many are saddened at Christmas time when they think of their loved ones who are not able to be there for various reasons. Christmas dinners may be only a wish and not a reality for some.

Yet, Christmas can be a season of great joy, a time when we think of those who are dear to us, when we share gifts. And, especially it is a time when we remember the great love God has for us. You see, Christmas is when we celebrate the birth of the Christ child. God sent His Son, Jesus, into the world to be born. Jesus is the reason for the season!

Introductory Rites

Carol

O Come all Ye Faithful

Oh, come, all ye faithful,
Joyful and triumphant!
Oh, come ye, oh, come ye to Bethlehem;
Come and behold him
Born the king of angels:
Oh, come, let us adore him,
Oh, come, let us adore him,
Oh, come, let us adore him,
Christ the Lord.

Highest, most holy,
Light of light eternal,
Born of a virgin,
A mortal he comes;
Son of the Father
Now in flesh appearing!
Oh, come, let us adore him,
Oh, come, let us adore him,
Oh, come, let us adore him,
Christ the Lord.

Sing, choirs of angels,
Sing in exultation,
Sing, all ye citizens of heaven above!
Glory to God
In the highest:
Oh, come, let us adore him,
Oh, come, let us adore him,
Oh, come, let us adore him,
Christ the Lord.

Yea, Lord, we greet thee,
Born this happy morning;
Jesus, to thee be glory given!
Word of the Father,
Now in flesh appearing!
Oh, come, let us adore him,
Oh, come, let us adore him,
Oh, come, let us adore him,
Christ the Lord.

Opening Prayer

> Leader: My friends, today we gather to remember and give thanks for Jesus, our Emmanuel, who promises to be with us always. Let us pray ...

(A large prominent white candle could be lit at this time / during the reading of the prayer.)

> Reader: We praise you, gracious God, for the glad tidings of peace, the good news of salvation; your Word became flesh, and we have seen his glory.
>
> Let the radiance of that glory enlighten the lives of those who celebrate his birth. Reveal to all the world the light no darkness can extinguish, our Lord Jesus Christ, who lives and reigns with you in the unity of the Holy Spirit, in the splendor of eternal light, God for ever and ever.

> *All: Amen.*

Penitential Rite/Confession

> Leader: Return to the Lord your God, who is gracious and merciful, slow to anger, and abounding in steadfast love. Let us now confess our sins to almighty God.

(PAUSE)

> *All:* *Heavenly Father, you have loved us with an everlasting love, but we have broken your holy laws and have left undone what we ought to have done.*
> *We are sorry for our sins and turn away from them.*
>
> *For the sake of your Son who died for us, forgive us, cleanse us and change us.*
> *By your Holy Spirit,*

enable us to live for you; through Jesus Christ our Lord.
Amen.

God desires that none should perish, but that all should
turn to Christ, and live.
In response to his call we acknowledge our sins.
God pardons those who humbly repent, and truly believe
the gospel.
Therefore we have peace with God, through Jesus Christ.
Amen.

The Word of God

First Reading

Leader/Reader: A reading from the Prophet Isaiah, Chapter
9, Verses 1 to 7.

Nevertheless, there will be no more gloom for those
who were in distress. In the past he humbled the land
of Zebulun and the land of Naphtali, but in the future
he will honour Galilee of the nations, by the Way of
the Sea, beyond the Jordan—

The people walking in darkness
have seen a great light;
on those living in the land of deep darkness
a light has dawned.
You have enlarged the nation
and increased their joy;
they rejoice before you
as people rejoice at the harvest,
as soldiers rejoice
when dividing the plunder.
For as in the day of Midian's defeat,

you have shattered
the yoke that burdens them,
the bar across their shoulders,
the rod of their oppressor.
 Every warrior's boot used in battle
and every garment rolled in blood
will be destined for burning,
will be fuel for the fire.
For to us a child is born,
to us a son is given,
and the government will be on his shoulders.
And he will be called
Wonderful Counsellor, Mighty God,
Everlasting Father, Prince of Peace.
Of the increase of his government and peace
there will be no end.
He will reign on David's throne
and over his kingdom,
establishing and upholding it
with justice and righteousness
from that time on and forever.
The zeal of the LORD Almighty
will accomplish this.
This is the word of the Lord.

All: Thanks be to God.

Responsorial Psalm

Leader/Reader: All the ends of the earth have seen the saving
power of God.

All respond: All the ends of the earth have seen the saving power of God.
(Repeat after each verse)

1. Sing a new song to the Lord for he has worked wonders.
His right hand and his holy arm have brought salvation. *(R)*

2. The Lord has made known his salvation; has shown his justice to the nations.
He has remembered his truth and love for the house of Israel. *(R.)*

3. All the ends of the earth have seen the salvation of our God.
Shout to the Lord all the earth, ring out your joy. *(R)*

4. Sing psalms to the Lord with the harp, with the sound of music. With trumpets and the sound of the horn acclaim the King, the Lord. *(R.)*

Second Reading

Leader/Reader: A Reading from the Letter of Paul to Titus, Chapter 3, Versus 4 to 7.

But when the kindness and love of God our Saviour appeared, he saved us, not because of righteous things we had done, but because of his mercy. He saved us through the washing of rebirth and renewal by the Holy Spirit, whom he poured out on us generously through Jesus Christ our Saviour, so that, having been justified by his grace, we might become heirs having the hope of eternal life.

This is the Word of the Lord.

All: *Thanks be to God.*

Gospel Reading

Leader/Reader: A reading from the Holy Gospel according to Luke, Chapter 2, versus 1 to 14.

In those days Caesar Augustus issued a decree that a census should be taken of the entire Roman world. (This was the first census that took place while Quirinius was governor of Syria.) And everyone went to their own town to register.

So Joseph also went up from the town of Nazareth in Galilee to Judea, to Bethlehem the town of David, because he belonged to the house and line of David. He went there to register with Mary, who was pledged to be married to him and was expecting a child. While they were there, the time came for the baby to be born, and she gave birth to her firstborn, a son. She wrapped him in cloths and placed him in a manger, because there was no guest room available for them.

And there were shepherds living out in the fields nearby, keeping watch over their flocks at night. An angel of the Lord appeared to them, and the glory of the Lord shone around them, and they were terrified. But the angel said to them, "Do not be afraid. I bring you good news of great joy that will be for all the people. Today in the town of David a Saviour has been born to you; he is the Messiah, the Lord. This will be a sign to you: You will find a baby wrapped in cloths and lying in a manger."

Suddenly a great company of the heavenly host appeared with the angel, praising God and saying,

"Glory to God in the highest heaven, and on earth peace to those on whom his favour rests."

When the angels had left them and gone into heaven, the shepherds said to one another, 'Let's go to Bethlehem and see this thing that has happened, which the Lord has told us about.'

So they hurried off and found Mary and Joseph, and the baby, who was lying in the manger. When they had seen him, they spread the word concerning what had been told them about this child, and all who heard it were amazed at what the shepherds said to them. But Mary treasured up all these things and pondered them in her heart. The shepherds returned, glorifying and praising God for all the things they had heard and seen, which were just as they had been told.

This is the Gospel of the Lord.

All: Praise and Glory to you Lord Jesus Christ.

Quiet Reflection

Everyone is invited to spend a minute or two in quiet reflection. Questions you might like to ponder might include:
- What is the real meaning of Christmas for me?
- Jesus asked his disciples, 'Who do you say I am?' ... what would my answer be?
- How can I bring the spirit of Christmas into my life throughout the year?
- How am I called to deepen my faith in the year ahead?

Carol: Hark the Herald Angels Sing

Hark the herald angels sing
'Glory to the newborn King!
Peace on earth and mercy mild
God and sinners reconciled'
Joyful, all ye nations rise
Join the triumph of the skies
With the angelic host proclaim:
'Christ is born in Bethlehem'
Hark! The herald angels sing
'Glory to the newborn King!'

Christ by highest heav'n adored
Christ the everlasting Lord!
Late in time behold Him come
Offspring of a Virgin's womb
Veiled in flesh the Godhead see
Hail the incarnate Deity
Pleased as man with man to dwell
Jesus, our Emmanuel
Hark! The herald angels sing
'Glory to the newborn King!'

Hail the heav'n-born Prince of Peace!
Hail the Son of Righteousness!
Light and life to all He brings
Ris'n with healing in His wings
Mild He lays His glory by
Born that man no more may die
Born to raise the sons of earth
Born to give them second birth
Hark! The herald angels sing
'Glory to the newborn King!'

The faith and prayers of the community

Affirmation of Faith: The Apostles Creed

All: *I believe in God, the Father almighty,*
creator of heaven and earth.

I believe in Jesus Christ his only Son, our Lord,
who was conceived by the Holy Spirit,
born of the Virgin Mary,
suffered under Pontius Pilate,
was crucified, died, and was buried;
On the third day he rose again;
he ascended into heaven,
he is seated at the right hand of the Father,
and he will come to judge the living and the dead.

I believe in the Holy Spirit,
the holy catholic Church,
the communion of saints,
the forgiveness of sins,
the resurrection of the body,
and the life everlasting.
Amen.

Prayers of Intercession

Leader: Let us join our prayers to the prayers of believers
everywhere and intercede for our world, as we pray ...

R. Lord hear our prayer ...

For the Christian churches; that our leaders, our
communities and each one of us individually may
witness to the presence of God in our world ...
We pray ...

R. Lord hear our prayer ...

For the world; that all nations may find paths to peace ...
We pray ...

R. *Lord hear our prayer ...*

For the families of all those gathered here, and for families everywhere; that life together may be marked by kindness, gentleness, patience, self-control, affection and good humour ...
We pray ...

R. *Lord hear our prayer ...*

For those who are struggling; that those experiencing hardship or pain at this time may know of God's love and care for them ... We pray ...

R. *Lord hear our prayer ...*

We remember those who have died; for all members of our families and of this community who have gone before us ... We pray ...

R. *Lord hear our prayer ...*

The Lord's Prayer

Leader: Mindful of God's gracious bounty we pray.

All: *Our Father in heaven.*
Hallowed be your name,
Your kingdom come,
Your will be done,
On earth as in heaven.

Give us today our daily bread
Forgive us our sins
As we forgive those who sin against us.
Save us from the time of trial

And deliver us from evil.
For the kingdom, the power
And the glory are yours
Now and for ever. Amen.

Sign of Peace

Leader: Sisters and brothers, Let us share the sign of peace.

Concluding Rites

Closing Prayer

Leader: Father the child born today is the Saviour of the
World.
He made us your children.
May He welcome us into your Kingdom
Where He lives and reigns with you for ever and ever.
Amen

Blessing and Dismissal

Leader: May the God of hope fill us with every joy in
believing.
May the peace of Christ abound in our hearts.
May the Holy Spirit enrich us with his gifts,
now and forever.

All: Amen.

Leader Let us go forth in the peace of Christ.

All: Thanks be to God.

Carol: Joy to the World

Joy to the World , the Lord is come!
Let earth receive her King;
Let every heart prepare Him room,
And Heaven and nature sing,
And Heaven and nature sing,
And Heaven, and Heaven, and nature sing.

Joy to the World, the Saviour reigns!
Let men their songs employ;
While fields and floods, rocks, hills and plains
Repeat the sounding joy,
Repeat the sounding joy,
Repeat, repeat, the sounding joy.

He rules the world with truth and grace,
And makes the nations prove
The glories of His righteousness,
And wonders of His love,
And wonders of His love,
And wonders, wonders, of His love.

APPENDIX D
EASTER LITURGY SOME
SUGGESTIONS

Overview

Easter, which celebrates the resurrection of Jesus, is the most important day of the year for all Christians. As St. Paul rightly pointed out nearly 2,000 years ago, without the resurrection, Christian faith is baseless. At the same time, it is important to hold both the death—by crucifixion—of Jesus, and His resurrection, in view at the same time as too much focus on one or the other distorts the Good News of the Gospels and thus the witness and the mission of Jesus himself. Too much emphasis on his horrific death, sacrifice and suffering can lead to what might be referred to as 'Good Friday Christians', while too much emphasis on the events of Easter Sunday can lead to a view of Christianity that might be referred to as 'Cargo-cult Christianity', that focuses on blessings and minimises the fact that suffering is indeed part of Jesus' story and is also involved in taking up our crosses and following in His footsteps.

This presents some challenges in developing an Easter Liturgy which brings both elements into view. But these are not insurmountable and can be mostly accommodated with an appropriate setting or arrangement, a careful selection of readings (see below) and some guided sharing/reflections around the twin themes of Jesus' death and resurrection.

The liturgy format at Appendix A should also be used for Easter.

Ideally the place of gathering should be around a specially prepared table or space, spread with a white cloth. The centre piece should ideally be a Bible which might be opened at one of the readings of this service. Other items that could be placed on the cloth might include a cross, some candles and flowers, and if available, an Easter egg. There should also be copies of the Liturgy at Appendix A so that all can follow along.

Welcome The leader or host welcomes everyone present.

Leader/Reader: Today we gather together to celebrate Easter, the most important day of the year for all Christians throughout the whole world. It is the day on which we commemorate the resurrection of Jesus, meaning that His body and soul came back to life after He had been killed in a truly horrible way, by being nailed to a cross, what we know as being *crucified*, a few days before. These events are central to Christian faith and beliefs.

All this happened nearly 2,000 years ago, however, the death and resurrection of Jesus forever changed the lives of those who knew Him and had followed Him for about three years. Many of these disciples were radically changed and became fearless witnesses to what became known as Christianity. Not only that, but nearly all of them were so convinced of the truth of what had happened with Jesus that they were prepared to die for their beliefs, and many of them did.

Today, we are invited to consider our individual responses as Christians and perhaps to challenge ourselves to be better followers of Jesus, to start afresh if we need to, to be better people and more loving and compassionate just as Jesus was, especially for those who were sick or poor or otherwise disadvantaged. Easter is a time of new beginnings and also for us to renew our faith that Easter Sunday always follows Good Friday; that our own times of difficulty and strife or troubles will never have the last word, to hope that Our Father in heaven will see us through these times, just as He did for Jesus.

Please now follow the liturgy format at Appendix A and use the following readings:

First Reading: (from 1st Letter of Paul to the Corinthians Chapter 15)

Now I would remind you, brothers and sisters, of the good news that I proclaimed to you, which you in turn received, in which also you stand, through which also you are being saved, if you hold firmly to the message that I proclaimed to you—unless you have come to believe in vain.

For I handed on to you as of first importance what I in turn had received: that Christ died for our sins in accordance with the scriptures, and that he was buried, and that he was raised on the third day in accordance with the scriptures, and that he appeared to Cephas, then to the twelve. Then he appeared to more than five hundred brothers and sisters at one time, most of whom are still alive, though some have died. Then he appeared to James, then to all the apostles. Last of all, as to one untimely born, he appeared also to me.

...Now if Christ is proclaimed as raised from the dead, how can some of you say there is no resurrection of the dead? If there is no resurrection of the dead, then Christ has not been raised; and if Christ has not been raised, then our proclamation has been in vain and your faith has been in vain.

Responsorial Psalm

Response: This is the day the Lord has made; let us rejoice and be glad.

> Give thanks to the LORD, for he is good,
> for his mercy endures forever.
> Let the house of Israel say,
> 'His mercy endures forever.'

Response: This is the day the Lord has made; let us rejoice and be glad.

> The right hand of the LORD has struck with power;
> the right hand of the LORD is exalted.
> I shall not die, but live,
> and declare the works of the LORD.

Response. This is the day the Lord has made; let us rejoice and be glad.

> The stone which the builders rejected
> has become the cornerstone.
> By the LORD has this been done;
> it is wonderful in our eyes.

Response. This is the day the Lord has made; let us rejoice and be glad.

Second Reading (from the Acts of the Apostles, Chapter 3)

> Peter said to the people, The God of Abraham, the God
> of Isaac, and the God of Jacob, the God of our fathers, has
> glorified his servant Jesus, whom you handed over and denied
> in Pilate's presence when he had decided to release him.

> You denied the Holy and Righteous One and asked that
> a murderer be released to you. The author of life you put
> to death, but God raised him from the dead; of this we
> are witnesses. Now I know, brothers, that you acted out of
> ignorance, just as your leaders did; but God has thus brought
> to fulfilment what he had announced beforehand through

the mouth of all the prophets, that his Christ would suffer.

Repent, therefore, and be converted, that your sins may be wiped away.

This is the Word of the Lord.

Gospel Acclamation:

Alleluia, alleluia.
Christ, our paschal lamb, has been sacrificed;
let us then feast with joy in the Lord.
R. *Alleluia, alleluia.*

Gospel

A reading from the Holy Gospel according to John, Chapter 20, verses 1-9.

On the first day of the week, Mary of Magdala came to the tomb early in the morning, while it was still dark, and saw the stone removed from the tomb.

So she ran and went to Simon Peter and to the other disciple whom Jesus loved, and told them,

'They have taken the Lord from the tomb, and we don't know where they put him.'

So Peter and the other disciple went out and came to the tomb.

They both ran, but the other disciple ran faster than Peter and arrived at the tomb first;

he bent down and saw the burial cloths there, but did not go in.

When Simon Peter arrived after him, he went into the tomb and saw the burial cloths there, and the cloth that had covered his head, not with the burial cloths but rolled up in a separate place.

Then the other disciple also went in, the one who had arrived at the tomb first, and he saw and believed.

For they did not yet understand the Scripture that he had to rise from the dead.

This is the Gospel of the Lord.

Some Possible Themes for Shared Reflection on the readings:

- Why Easter eggs? They can be a symbol of new life, breaking out of the shell as Jesus coming out of the tomb etc.
- What it would have been like on that first Easter morning for Mary of Magdala, and Simon Peter? How might this incredible experience have changed their lives?
- How important is Easter for your faith? Do you agree with Paul that without the resurrection our faith would be in vain?
- Peter described himself as one of the witnesses to the Risen Christ. Do we believe his testimony? And if so, how does this belief influence the way we live our lives?
- Can we share about how, after our prayers during a terrible experience, all was well again? Can we relate this to what happened to Jesus?
- How do you feel about Jesus conquering death by His resurrection? How does this event apply to your own death?

APPENDIX E
PRAYING WITH THE DYING

Please feel very free to use as much or as little of this prayer service as you consider appropriate for your circumstances.

Short Texts

You might like to softly recite (and/or repeat) one or more of these short texts with or for the dying person.

To you Lord I lift up my soul (Psalm 25:1).

The Lord is my light and my salvation (Psalm 27:1).

Into your hands Lord, I commend my spirit (Psalm 31:5a).

Readings

You might like to read one or more of the following:

The Lord is my Shepherd (Psalm 23)

The Lord is my shepherd, I lack nothing.

He makes me lie down in green pastures,

he leads me beside quiet waters,

he refreshes my soul.

He guides me along the right paths

for his name's sake.

Even though I walk

through the darkest valley,

I will fear no evil,

for you are with me;

your rod and your staff,

they comfort me.

You prepare a table before me

in the presence of my enemies.

You anoint my head with oil;

my cup overflows.

Surely your goodness and love will follow me

all the days of my life,

and I will dwell in the house of the Lord

forever.

The Resurrection of Jesus (Luke 24:1-8)

But on the first day of the week, at early dawn, they came to the tomb, taking the spices that they had prepared. They found the stone rolled away from the tomb, but when they went in, they did not find the body. While they were perplexed about this, suddenly two men in dazzling clothes stood beside them. The women were terrified and bowed their faces to the ground, but the men said to them, 'Why do you look for the living among the dead? He is not here, but has risen. Remember how he told you, while he was still in Galilee, that the Son of Man must be handed over to sinners, and be crucified, and on the third day rise again'. Then they remembered his words,

Jesus the Way to the Father (John 14:1-6)

Do not let your hearts be troubled. Believe in God, believe also in me. In my Father's house there are many dwelling-places. If it were not so, would I have told you that I go to prepare a place for you? And if I go and prepare a place for

you, I will come again and will take you to myself, so that
where I am, there you may be also. And you know the way to
the place where I am going.

Thomas said to him, 'Lord, we do not know where you are
going. How can we know the way? Jesus said to him, 'I am
the way, and the truth, and the life. No one comes to the
Father except through me. If you know me, you will know
my Father also. From now on you do know him and have
seen him.

Future Glory (Romans 8)

I consider that the sufferings of this present time are not
worth comparing with the glory about to be revealed to us.

Likewise the Spirit helps us in our weakness; for we do
not know how to pray as we should, but that very Spirit
intercedes with sighs too deep for words. And God, who
searches the heart, knows what the mind of the Spirit is,
because the Spirit intercedes for the saints according to the
will of God.

We know that all things work together for good for those
who love God, who are called according to his purpose.

What then are we to say about these things? If God is for us,
who is against us? He who did not withhold his own Son,
but gave him up for all of us, will he not with him also give
us everything else? Who will separate us from the love of
Christ? Will hardship, or distress, or persecution, or famine,
or nakedness, or peril, or sword?

No, in all these things we are more than conquerors through
him who loved us. For I am convinced that neither death,
nor life, nor angels, nor rulers, nor things present, nor things

to come, nor powers, nor height, nor depth, nor anything
else in all creation, will be able to separate us from the love
of God in Christ Jesus our Lord.

Prayer of Commendation

When the moment of death seems near, this prayer can be used:
I commend you, my dear brother /sister, to almighty God,
and entrust you to your Creator. May you return to him who
formed you from the dust of the earth. May holy Mary, the
angels, and all the saints come to meet you as you go forth
from this life.

May Christ who was crucified for you bring you freedom
and peace. May Christ who died for you admit you into
his garden of paradise. May Christ, the true Shepherd,
acknowledge you as one of his flock. May he forgive all your
sins, and set you among those he has chosen. May you see
your Redeemer face to face, and enjoy the vision of God for
ever.

Amen.

Prayer after Death

Give him/her eternal rest O Lord, and may your light shine
on him/her forever.

Let us pray:

God of love
welcome into your presence
your son/daughter (Name) who you have called from this
life.
Release him/her from his/her sins
bless him/her with eternal light and peace,

raise him/her up to live forever with all your saints
in the glory of the resurrection.
We ask this through Christ our Lord. Amen.

Prayer for Family and Friends

Let us pray:

God of all consolation
in your unending love and mercy for us
you turn the darkness of death
into the dawn of new life.
Show compassion to your people in their sorrow.
Your Son, Our Lord Jesus Christ,
by dying for us conquered death
and by rising again, restored life.
May we then go forward eagerly to meet him,
and after our life on earth, be reunited with our brothers and
sisters
where every tear will be wiped away.
We ask this through Christ our Lord. Amen.

www.ingramcontent.com/pod-product-compliance
Lightning Source LLC
LaVergne TN
LVHW021121080426
835509LV00011B/1368